Sternwheelers On The Great Kanawha River

Gerald W. Sutphin

Richard A. Andre

Credits

West Virginia State Archives	WVSA
Wisconsia State Historical Society	WSHS
Inland Rivers Library, Public Library of Cincinnati and Hamilton County, Ohio	IRLC
Donald T. Wright Collection - Tulane University	DTW-TU

All photographs not credited are from the Steamboat Photo Collection of Gerald W. Sutphin.

Design and layout by Gerald W. Sutphin.

Dedication

To—

Mom and Dad
for the opportuunities...

Lenora, for your patience,
encouragement, and most of all,
love.

Jerry

Dedication

My Dad was born in Charleston in 1886. He grew up in that wonderful turn of the century America with its abundant miracles; the telephone, automobile, flying machine, radio, motion pictures. Dad loved the river as did all young men of the age for it was their playground and the great steamboats that ran upon it were as much a part of their lives as a Boeing jetliner is to the youth of today. I will always remember Dad's story of standing on the bank of the river and seeing his first glimpse of violent death as the bloated bodies of long submerged victims of the *Kanawha Belle* were pulled ashore at Charleston weeks after the wreck at Marmet.

I almost missed the steamboat because I was born in 1940 and by that time the passenger packets were a thing of the past except for the excursion boats that occasionally plied the river. In 1947 I was six years old and the fine old steamer *Gordon Greene* had come to town. Dad, bless his heart, knew that the chances of my ever riding an honest to god steamboat would grow slimmer with every passing day and, because he was wise and romantic, he asked my mother to "take Dickie for a ride on the *Gordon Greene*."

So I was privileged to spend a few hours on that wonderful river "Queen" and I have been hooked ever since on steamboats. A six-year-old boy is barely three feet tall and thus the old steamer looms large in my memory. The engine room I loved above all others for it was there that the giant's heart could be heard beating. The sweet smell of steam and the powerful yet somehow gentle breath as the intake and exhaust valves opened and closed captured my childish imagination and I went to sleep that night full of visions of great ships and far away places.

And so it is that I dedicate my part in this book to my Mom and Dad. To Dad for his great sense of history and to Mom for her patience in understanding.

Richard A. Andre

Contents

Acknowledgments

This book could never have been written or illustrated without the willing assistance and overwhelming generousity of a great many people.

From the day Jack C. Burdette of Point Pleasant, W. Va. surprised me by paying my first years dues in the Sons and Daughters of Pioneer Rivermen, it has been the people I have met and became friends with that have meant the most about my involvment with the river and steamboats.

There are those to whom I extend a special Thank You: Captain Frederick Way, Jr. and his wife Grace, and Captain C. W. Stoll and his wife Lucy who opened their homes to me and Lenora on too many occasions to remember, treating us as if we were members of their family. Captain Charles Henry Stone and Jean, our base of operations in Point Pleasant, W. Va. and Captain Clarke "Doc" Hawley, our New Orleans connection.

And the list goes on: Herschel W. Burford, R. Jerome Collins, Captain Ben Gilbert, James A. Wallen, Ralph R. DuPae, Bert Fenn, Alan L. Bates, Nelson Jones, Charles T. Jones, Captain Bill Barr, Jim Bupp, Captain Harold B. Wright, Captain Bert Shearer, Captain Harry White, John B. Briley, Jack E. Custer, L. F. "Dick" Sutherland, Jr., Mr. & Mrs. William R. Smith, Mrs. Catherine Remley, Jeffrey L. Spears, Keith E. Norrington, Dr. Leland R. Johnson, Ann Emich, Daniel E. Davidson, John and Marie Hartford, Mr. and Mrs. J. W. Rutter, Captain Thomas E. Kenny, James Harmon, William Wentz, M'Lissa Kesterman, Inland River Library, Public Library of Cincinnati and Hamilton County, Ohio, and Debra Basham, West Virginia State Archives.

To all of you and to those I know I have forgotten—Thank You and I hope you enjoy *Sternwheelers on the Great Kanawha River*.

Gerald W. Sutphin
August 30, 1991

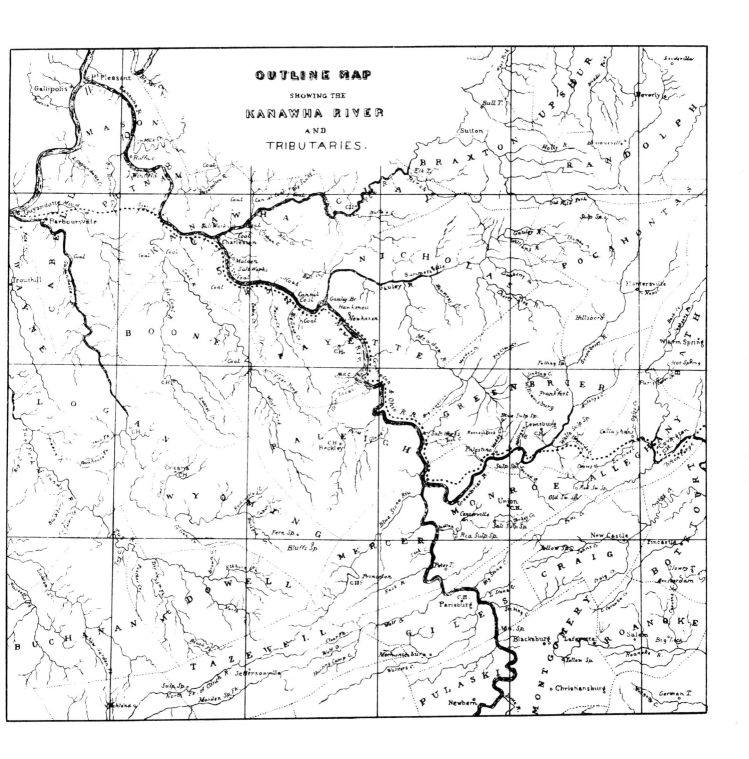

OUTLINE MAP

SHOWING THE

KANAWHA RIVER

AND

TRIBUTARIES.

Ancient River — Early Commerce

The Great Kanawha River lies wholly within the State of West Virginia from its formation at Gauley Bridge with the meeting of the New River and the Gauley River to its emptying in the Ohio River 97 miles downstream at Point Pleasant.

With the New River originating in the mountains of northwestern North Carolina and the Gauley River beginning in the northeastern highlands of West Virginia, Virginia, and North Carolina. Other major streams adding their water to the Great Kanawha are the Bluestone, Greenbrier, Elk, Coal and Pocatalico Rivers.

At Kanawha Falls, about a mile below the head of the river, there is a drop of 15 feet. From the basin of the falls to the mouth of the river, a distance of 96 miles, the total fall is 108 feet.

The Great Kanawha is an extension of what is considered by many to be one of the oldest rivers on earth; the New River. The New River is actually a remaining part of a much greater prehistoric river known by geologists as the Teays River. Draining essentially the same areas as those drained by the Ohio and Mississippi rivers today, the Teays was formed well over 100,000,000 years ago. It is more than 1,000 miles long, extending from North Carolina northwest across Virginia, West Virginia, Ohio, Indiana, and Illinois. Turning south it then flows south toward the Gulf of Mexico.

When the last great ice age occurred, the glaciers moved as far south as the southern most tip of Illinois and created a hugh dam across the rivers as shown in the map. The upper section of the Teays River, from its source in North Carolina to above Chillicothe, Ohio became the lake formed by this dam.

With the warming of the earth and the glacial ice receding, the course of the Teays River changed while other rivers were being established. Its headwaters, that part from North Carolina to about Nitro, West Virginia, remained to become what is now the New and the upper Great Kanawha rivers. The Teays abandoned its old streambed between Nitro and Huntington, West Virginia and between Portsmouth and Chillicothe, Ohio while its waters established the lower course of the Great Kanawha where it emptied into the newly formed Ohio River.

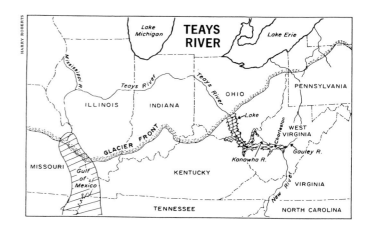

The name Kanawha, usually pronounced "Ka-gnaw-wa" with the accent on the "gnaw" is generally accepted to have been the name of an Indian tribe that once dwelt along the Potomac and westward to Wood's or New River. It has been spelled many different ways. Wyman's map of the British Empire in 1770 calls it the "Great Conoway or Wood's river." The act of the Virginia Legislature, in 1788-89, establishing the county, spelled it Kanawha. In an original report of a survey near the mouth of the river, made by Daniel Boone in 1791, he spelled it "Conhawway". At different times it has also been spelled, "Conoys, Conoise, Canawese, Conhawas, Canaways and Kenhawas".

"Chi-na-do-chetha" was the name given to the river on August 18, 1749 when French engineer Captain DeCeleron and his men buried a leaden plate at its mouth claiming all the territory drained by its waters for the French crown.

Evidence of early man's presence along the Great Kanawha River can easily be traced to ancient cultures by archaeological finds. The most popular of these is the Adena mound at South Charleston. However, there are many other lesser known evidences of these ancient civilizations within the valley.

One of the most interesting of these ancient finds is the wall on Loup Creek Mountain. The Loup Creek Wall is built of flag-stones without any mortar and without arranged foundation.

The wall extends along the top of the mountain from Armstrong's Creek to Loup Creek. It commences on the west side of the mountain, fronting on the river, above Armstrong's Creek about one hundred yards from the top of the mountain and follows the meandering of the ridge, until it reaches that slope that extends down the Loup Creek, near the Big Falls. Built of flag-stones, the entire length of the wall is about three and one half miles long. Early accounts estimate the wall six or seven feet high, two feet wide at the base and with a number of openings or gates. Speculation concerning the use of the wall and its age vary but the descendants of William Morris, the first permanent settler in Kanawha County, who settled in the vicinity of this wall in 1774 claim that he was told by the Indians that the wall was there when they arrived in the valley.

The 1894 Twelfth Annual Report of Mound Explorations by the Bureau of Ethnology reports, "along the Kanawha River from 3 to 8 miles below Charleston are the most extensive and interesting ancient works to be found in the State of West Virginia." The report states that there were fifty mounds varying in diameter from 35 to 200 feet and from 3 to 35 feet in height in this area. Artifacts found in the mounds at the time of examination revealed a great deal about the way these ancient cultures lived, ate, hunted, fished and buried their dead.

It is not known how or when these ancient cultures left the Kanawha valley but when the first settlers moved into the valley in the late 1700's only a few Shawnees remained. These Shawnees represented the culture that had moved into the valley sometime after the ancient culture had disappeared. All of these early inhabitants used the river for a source of food and travel. The canoe was the prime means by which this travel was accomplished. The canoe used on the Kanawha was a dugout canoe usually made of large poplar trees, made light and thin and rounded to a point on both ends. These sturdy boats were used to carry supplies as well as to travel from one point to another.

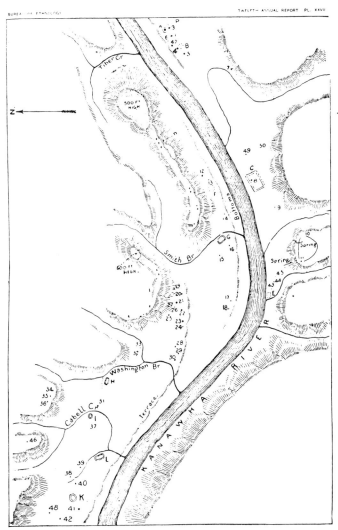

PLAT OF GROUP NEAR CHARLESTON, KANAWHA COUNTY, WEST VIRGINIA.

DANIEL BOONE.

As the white man moved into the Kanawha River valley, its waters reflected the campfire of such well known historic figures as the great Shawnee Chief Cornstalk, Daniel Boone, Simon Kenton, George Washington, Andrew Lewis as well as Mary Draper Ingles, during her period of captivity by the Shawnees in 1755.

In July 1755, a Shawnee war party took Mrs. Mary Ingles and Mrs. Bettie Draper prisoners after killing or wounding the settlers in Draper's Meadows (Virginia) on the New River. Traveling down the New River with their plunder and prisoners, the Indians changed course near the Bluestone River to cross Flat Top Mountain. After descending Paint Creek, the Shawnees continued the journey down the Kanawha River stopping only at the mouth of Campbell's Creek to gather game and make salt.

The Indians and their captives continued down the Kanawha and then down the Ohio to the mouth of the Scioto River. Later while again making salt for the captor at Big Bone Lick in Boone County, Kentucky, Mary Ingles escaped and eventually found her way back to Draper's Meadows.

Her remarkable journey at the hands of the Shawnees made Mary Ingles the first white woman in both the Great Kanawha and Ohio River valleys. She was also the first white person to engage in the making of salt on the Kanawha; a practice that was to become the valley's first industry.

In 1878 the Annual Report of the Chief of Engineers, Dr. Hale Piece, to the Secretary of War for the Year 1877 provided an insight into the importance of the production of salt in the development of the Kanawha River. The report states the following: "The Kanawha salt-works are situated in Kanawha County on the Kanawha River commencing about three miles above Charleston and extending up river for several miles on both sides. From the 2,000 or 3,000 or 4,000 bushels per month of the earlier furnaces, the production has been increased to 20,000, 30,000 or 40,000 bushels per month... How far this will be exceeded in the future remains to be seen. The same progress has occurred in freighting salt as in the manufacture. In the days of Elisha Brooks, the neighbors took the salt from the kettles in their pocket handkerchiefs, tin-buckets or pillowcases. Later it was taken in meal bags, on packhorse and pack-saddles. The first shipment west by river was in 1808, in tubs, boxes, and hogsheads, floated on a raft of logs. Next came small flat-boats, 50 to 75 feet long, and 18 to 20 feet wide, run by hand, and in which salt was shipped in barrels. These boats increased in size up to 160 feet or more long and 24 to 25 feet wide, and carried 1,800 to 2,200 barrels of salt. These boats were all run by hand, at a great risk, and although the Kanawha boatmen were the best in the world, the boats and cargoes were frequently sunk, entailing heavy loss upon the owners of the salt. The late Col. Andrew Donnally used to ask, when he heard of one of his boats sinking, whether any of the boatmen were drowned; if not, he contended it was not a fair sink. But all this is now done away with. Salt is now shipped eastward by rail, and to the nearer westward markets by daily and weekly steamboat packets, and to the most distant markets by tow-boats and barges. A tow-boat will now take 8,000 to 15,000 barrels at a trip, landing them at Louisville, Evansville, Nashville, Memphis, Saint Louis or elsewhere.

This same report listed ten of the most prominent Kanawha salt-furnaces with such colorful names as Daniel Boone, Snow Hill, Burning Springs, Lorena and Kenton. Production of salt ranges from approximately 150 pounds per day in 1797 to 2,951,492 bushels in 1849 to 1,721,963 bushels in 1870. The 1877 Corps of Engineer Annual Report chronicles events and incidents that relate to salt production and the development of transportation on the Kanawha Rivers as follows:

"1774 - Walter Kelly and family first white settlers in the Kanawha Valley.

1785 - John Dickenson 'located' the Kanawha salt-springs.

1808 - First salt shipped west by river in tubs and boxes on a log-raft and in canoes.

1816 - First steamboat ever in Kanawha, called the *Eliza*.*

1817 - Coal first used in salt-making.

1817 - First Kanawha salt company, "Steel, Donnally & Steele."

1822 - Highest water ever known in Kanawha to that time.

1843 - Big Burning Spring gas-well struck.

1856 - Lowest water ever known on the Kanawha and Ohio Rivers.

1856-57 - Coldest winter and longest freeze-up ever known on the Kanawha.

1861 - Disastrous flood in the river; the highest water ever known on the Kanawha.

1861-65 - War

1872 - The Chesapeake and Ohio Railroad opened.

*(See Chapter 2).

1875 - The ninth and present salt company 'The Kanawha Salt Company' organized.

1875 - United States Government commenced to improve the Kanawha River by locks and dams."

1832 bill of lading for the keelboat *Simon* carrying freight from Pittsburgh to Charleston.

HANNA & POINDEXTER,
Wholesale Grocers and Commission Merchants,
No. 7, Market Street, Pittsburgh.

SHIPPED

In good order, and well conditioned, by HANNA & POINDEXTER, on board the good *Keel* Boat called the *Simon*, whereof *Kounty* is master for the present voyage, now lying at the Port of Pittsburgh, and bound for *Kanawha, Va* the following articles, marked and numbered as below, which are to be delivered, without delay, in like good order, at the port of *Charleston, Va* (the unavailable dangers of the River only excepted,) unto *N. B. Coleman & Co.* or to *their assigns*; he or they to pay freight for the said goods, at the rate of *fifty* cents *per 100.*

IN WITNESS WHEREOF, The Owner, Master or Clerk of said boat has affirmed to *2* bills of lading, all of this tenor and date, one of which being accomplished, the other to stand void. Dated at Pittsburgh, this *20th* day of *April* 1832

Marked				
N. B. Coleman & Co.	1 Box Mdse.	383	Amt. Brot. forwd.	5093
Charleston	1 do do	457	1 Hhd. Queensware	600
Kanawha Va	1 Cask Hardware	474	1 Box Mdse	362
	1 do do	532	1 do do	201
	5 bundles Scythe in 2 packages	176	1 Hhd. Queensware	530
			1 Box Mdse	434

In the late 1790's, Kelly's Station on the Kanawha was a major flatboat building and embarkation point for hundreds of trans-allegheny pioneer in their move west. Many other boat building sites were located along the upper river and were kept busy building flatboats as well as salt boats. These salt boats were built in two sizes to transport the highly valued Kanawha "red salt", discolored by iron impurities, to the lower Ohio River valley where it was used for curing meats. The largest salt boats were one hundred feet long by twenty-five feet wide and seven feet high while the smaller revision was sixty feet long, fifteen feet wide and five feet in height. In 1829 the salt works required more than 300 salt boats to ship the Kanawha salt south.

The men who worked these salt boats, "poled" them down the river. The large salt boats had a crew of seven including the captain while the smaller boats had a crew of five. These men developed a reputation for reliability and hard work that was respected by all along the Kanawha and Ohio. It was a matter of record that when a river captain undertook to deliver a consignment, he did so or sank his boat. Many a load of salt has been sunk when the river was too high or the snags too numerous to make a landing.

Kanawha boatmen fulfilled their obligations and in turn expected others to fulfill theirs as well. This is illustrated by the fact that after delivering their salt boats near the mouth of the Cumberland river about 1837 a group of Kanawha boatmen chartered the small steamboat *Dove* to take them back to the Salines. The *Dove* brought them as far as Louisville where the captain found that he could do a more lucrative business than to make a trip to the Kanawha River. After informing his passengers that he would not take them any further than Louisville the boatmen quietly arrested the captain and his crew, placed them in close confinement and elected a complement of officers from their own members. After arriving in Charleston, the boat crew was released and the boat was permitted to return to the lower Ohio.

These same Kanawha boatmen were famous for their stone throwing. The stones along the river

WVSA

RIVER SCENE SHOWING FLATBOAT AND TWO KEELBOATS

were known as "the boatman's artillery" and the boatmen called themselves the "limestone artillerymen". How this art of throwing stones started and became associated with the Kanawha boatmen is not known but they gained a national reputation for the accuracy with which they threw them.

During this same period keelboats were also navigating the Kanawha taking passengers and trade goods both downstream and upstream. The trip downstream was difficult enough for the crewmen. Dodging snags, sandbars, boulders and other natural river hazards was hard work while floating downstream with the current but doing this while trying to propel the boat upstream was extremely arduous.

In 1817, Loammi Baldwin made an examination of the Kanawha River for the Board of Public Works for the Commonwealth of Virginia to determine what would need to be done to improve navigation. In addressing the keelboat operating on the river, Mr. Baldwin states: "The boats now in use in the Kanawha, and which also navigate the Ohio and Mississippi, are constructed with keels, drawing 2 to 3½ feet of water, and carry from 25 to 40 tons."... In descending, the keel boats are rowed, or shoved, and over some of the shoals pilots are taken on board to navigate them. This is usually done in descending Elk, Two Mile, and Island Shoals. In coming up, the boat is kept along the banks of the river, and the boatmen walk on the top, take hold of the brush and draw the boat forward, shoving with poles. The labor of shoving canoes is very difficult in ascending the channels of the shoals, where the water is shallow and the current very rapid. Barges, and some of the keel boats occasionally use large square sails when the wind blows up stream, with which they ascend even the shoals with surprising velocity."

In the 1826 report to the Board of Public Works, engineer C. Crozet referred to another type of boat used on the Kanawha. He states that most of the salt shipped is done in flat boats but that "some horse-boats are also used." Crozet concludes his report as follows: Horse-boats navigate the river now, and the time is probably not distance, when light steamboats will be able to ascend it. From the measurement I have taken of the velocity of the current at the most rapid sluices, and of which I have given an account in this report, it cannot be doubted that steamboats can steam it everywhere."

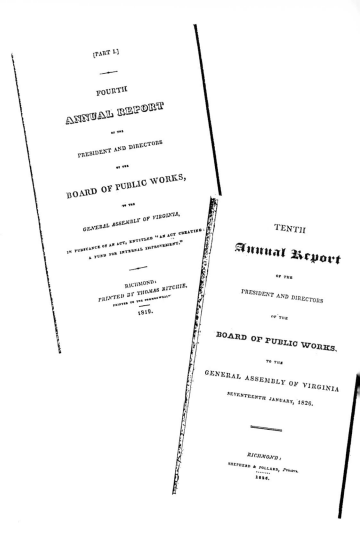

The Four Horse-Powered Boat

In the late 1840's, Captain Ben Wilson built a unique riverboat at Coalsmouth (St. Albans) on the Kanawha River. Although named the *Adventurer*, the boat came to be known as "Cap'n Ben Wilson's Horse Boat." Built specifically to carry a cargo of Kanawha River salt to New Orleans and return with a cargo of sugar and molasses, the boat measured 120 feet long and 18 feet wide. She had side wheels amidship and a rudder and rude tiller, that was operated by a pilot from a shed at the head of the boat boarded in on top to protect him from the weather. What made this boat so unusual was the fact that it

was powered by four horses walking on a tread wheel. The horses were attached to a long pole, one end of which was secured to a beveled cogwheel that engaged another cogwheel on the shaft of the paddle wheels. The horses went around in a circle, much in the fashion of a cane mill press, turning the paddle wheels of the boat.

With one captain and four crewmen and, of course, four horses, "Cap'n Ben Wilson's Horse Boat" left Coalsmouth in early April, 1848 with a load of salt for New Orleans. On October 21st, the *Adventurer* was back home to Coalsmouth with a full cargo of

molasses, which sold for $1.25 a gallon and sugar that was sold for 25 cents a pound. The trip had proved to be a very profitable one for Captain Ben. After spending over six months walking on the circular treadwheel, the horses were observed walking in a circle when turned out to pasture.

This turned out to be the one and only trip for the *Adventurer* because she was wrenched and sunk by ice during the following winter. Thus ended the career of what appears to be one of America's few horse-powered packet-boats.

CHARLESTON

FRIDAY MORNING, JUNE 24, 1830.

Kanawha River Tolls.—The descending tolls collected during the quarter euding 15th May last, arising from 212,604 bushels of salt, at half a cent per bushel, amounted to $1,063 02

Ascending tolls, on miscellaneous articles, same time, 439,99

$1,503,01

Of the miscellaneous articles ascending, there were 66,679 lbs. of dry goods—14,865 lbs. of coffee—58,939 lbs. of sugar—176,024 lbs. of bacon—10 cwt. hemp—about 60 tons castings—upwards of 4 tons 5 cwt. iron—11,153 lbs. nails—283,500 staves and shingles—21,000 hoop poles—about 1,500 gallons whiskey, wine, &c., and about 11,000 bushels of corn, potatoes, beans, apples. &c.

Kanawha
Register
February 26, 1830

Ohio River horse treadmill ferry operated at Ripley, Ohio about 1885.
The Kanawha River horse ferry probably looked much like this.

July 1, 1839 James River and Kanawha Company five
dollar note showing portrait of George Washington
who was an early proponent of the James-Kanawha
Route.

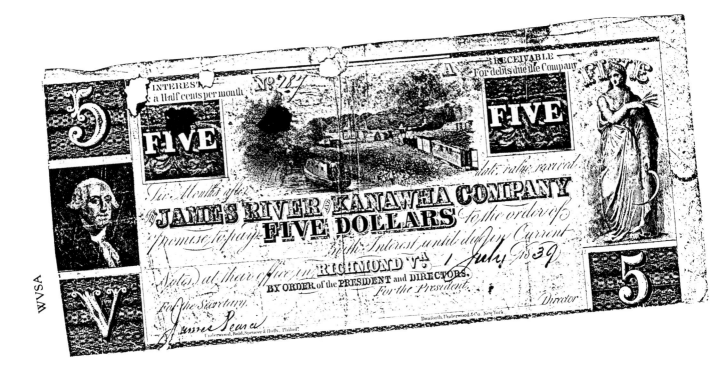

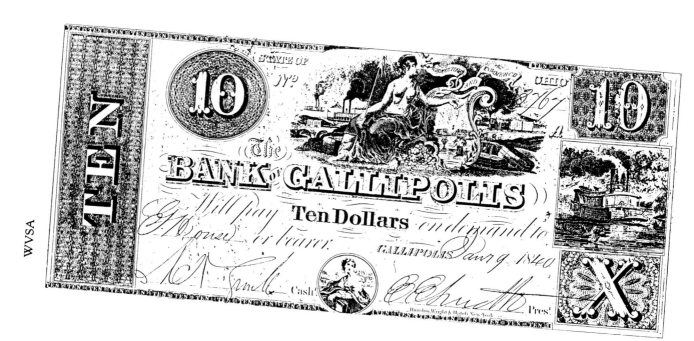

Note the illustration of the steamboat on the 1840
Bank of Gallipolis, Ohio ten dollar note. The use of
the steamboat reflects the importance of the boats to
the commerce and economy of the region.

Steam Comes To The Kanawha

On March 27, 1831, the *Kanawha Banner* announced the arrival of three keelboats at Charleston with cargos of oats, flour, potatoes, dried fruits, hoop-poles, staves and furniture. On April 2, Captain C. D. Knox arrived with his keelboat with cargo of corn and staves and on May 21, three more keelboats arrived with flour, corn, hoop-poles and staves. The sound of the keelboat captain's trumpet echoing off the valley hills was becoming a thing of the past because of the other boats sharing the landing.

The steamboats *Oliver H. Perry, Emigrant, Virginian, Criterion* and *Water Witch* carrying passengers and cargos of sugar, flour, bacon, whiskey and coffee also landed at Charleston during March and May of 1831. These boats had arrived from the towns of Cincinnati, Nashville and Frankfort, Kentucky carrying on regularly scheduled trades.

From the time the *New Orleans*, the first steamboat on the western rivers, had left Pittsburgh in 1811 for its destination of New Orleans, eight years had past before a steamboat had attempted to make its way up the Kanawha.

Although the first steamboat to travel the Kanawha's waters has been described as being a crude little barge-like boat with brick chimneys, the *Robert Thompson* was in reality a 65-foot-long side-wheel steamer with adventurers for owners. George A. Dohrman, Jacob A. Dohrman and Peter A. Dohrman built the *Thompson's* hull at Wellsville, Ohio and then moved it to their hometown, Steubenville, to put on the engines and cabin. A boat of a number of "first" on the western rivers, she was the first steamboat to have a double-flue boiler as all before her had been single-flue.

In 1819 the Dohrman boys attempted to take the *Thompson* up the Kanawha River to Charleston and above but were unable to get past the Red House Shoals. After waiting for a couple of days, the *Thompson* returned to the Ohio. The purpose of the *Thompson's* trip was to determine whether the Kanawha was navigable to Charleston. Because of the failure of the boat to reach its destination and the report of the boat's officers to the legislature of Virginia, a bill was passed in 1820 providing for improvements on the river.

Wheeling Gazette
April 14, 1821

STEAM BOAT NEWS.

The *Courier* arrived here on Monday last from Louisville, departed the same day for Pittsburgh—returned on Thursday, and left here yesterday for Louisville.

The *Robert Thompson* arrived here on Thursday from Pittsburgh, and departed the same day for Louisville.

The *Velocipede* arrived here yesterday from Louisville, and left here again for that place last evening.

The steamer *Robert Thompson* also had another first of note on the western rivers. After leaving Steubenville, Ohio in February 1822, she was the first steamboat up the Arkansas River when she delivered freight to Fort Smith, Arkansas.

Noted West Virginia historian John P. Hale, in his 1886 *Trans-Allegheny Pioneers*, states that in 1823 the *Eliza* was the first steamer to reach Charleston. However, in his 1891 *History of the Great Kanawha Valley*, Hale states "In December, 1820, the *Andrew Donnally*, a steamer built for Messrs. Andrew Donnally and Isaac Noyes, saltmakers of this neighborhood, made the first successful run to Charleston..."

Based on these dates, it appears that the *Andrew Donnally* was the first steamboat to succeed in reaching Charleston.

The sidewheeler steamer *Eliza* was built expressly for the Kanawha River and Wheeling salt trade by Messrs. Andrew Donnally and Isaac Noyes at a cost of $35,000. Her success at overcoming the Red House Shoals, the rivers' major obstacle, may have been due in part to the improvements that the State had performed in 1820 and 1821. Arriving at Charleston and proceeding upstream to the Salines, she was loaded out with salt and headed back downstream. After reaching the mouth of the Kanawha and starting up the Ohio River, the *Eliza* was unable to stem the current. At this point, Captain White, who

WHEELING:

FEBRUARY 15, 1820.

STEAM BOAT LAUNCH.

On Thursday last, the elegant steam boat ANDREW DONNELLY, of 230 tons, was launched from the boat yard of Mr. Geo. White. The regularity of movement from her wayes, and the safety with which she entered her designed element, drew forth the sentiments of unbounded satisfaction and applause from the attending multitude: in fact, her model and substantial workmanship together with the regular movement and safety of the launch, entitle the builder and his workmen to considerable merit.

Virginia Northwest Gazette
A Wheeling newspaper

Remarkable newspaper articles uncovered during research for this book describe the building of the *Andrew Donnally* which was the first steamboat to ascend the Kanawha to Charleston in 1820.

The 230-ton displacement of the *Donnally* indicate that she was a rather large and apparently first-class boat.

WHEELING:

FRIDAY, JUNE, 16, 1820.

STEAM BOAT NEWS.

The steam boat Wheeling Packet, lately built at Bridgeport, opposite this place, is now at our landing, undergoing some alterations, she will depart for Louisville in a few days.

The Andrew Donnelly is at Cincinnatti, receiving a new boiler, and is expected here shortly.

The Velocipede, is probably on her way up, her trip to and from Louisville, is generally performed in ten days. She made this place on her last passage up, in 100 hours running.

GAZETTE.

Wheeling, December 30.

The Steam Boat Donally, arrived here on Tuesday, last, from Kenhawa.

had brought her out from Wheeling, turned the boat downstream and proceeded to Cincinnati to sell his cargo of salt. The *Eliza* never returned to the Kanawha. She was remodeled at Cincinnati in the winter of 1822 and renamed the *Virginia*. There is some speculation that after leaving St. Louis in April, 1823, this *Virginia* was the first steamboat to reach the mouth of the Minnesota River. However, it should be noted that a number of boats were named or re-named *Virginia* during this period, including the *Andrew Donnally*, that also went to the upper Mississippi River area.

STEAM-BOAT NEWS.

The General Pike left here on Saturday last for Louisville

The Virginia, (formerly the Donally) left here yesterday for St. Louis.

The Wheeling Packet arrived here yesterday from Louisville.

Wheeling Gazette
March 17, 1821

Although these two earliest attempts for steamboats to conduct business on the Kanawha were not successful, the lucrative salt trade was reason enough for other attempts to be made. With each passing year improvements were being made to the methods of building steamboats and their machinery.

Andrew Donnally and A.M. Henderson had the steamer *Fairy Queen* built at Cincinnati in 1824 to become the first Charleston-Cincinnati packet. The *Fairy Queen* ran in this trade for several years and was joined by *Paul Pry* in 1826.

During the early 1830's, the Kanawha River was one of the most important natural tributaries of the Ohio River due to the Commonwealth of Virginia's project to connect the east with the west by the improved routing of the James River and the Kanawha River. The Kanawha Valley was the source of vast repository of natural resources that included timber, coal and salt. It was because

of all of this that the Kanawha became a natural area of business for enterprising rivermen.

The April 2, 1828 issue of *Western Virginian* announced the beginning of a new packet service between Cincinnati and Charleston that was to begin on April 15th. Built for Captain John Rogers and Joel Shrewsberry at Cincinnati, the new packet *Kanawha* appears to have been very successful in this trade as evidenced by her register on September 5, 1829 with the names of passengers from seven states including New York and Louisiana. The *Kanawha's* success was short lived as she was lost due to an explosion in 1829.

The New Steamboat

KANAWHA PACKET, designed as a regular weekly packet between Cincinnati and this place will be finished. & is expected here, on the 15th April. She will have comfortable accommodations for Cabin and Deck Passengers. Persons travelling on horseback, or in carriages, and movers, will be taken on board at Samuel Shrewsbury's, Col. D Ruffner's, and at Charleston; and will be landed at Cincinnati, or at any intermediate port.—Charges will be moderate. *Apply to*
ROGERS & SHREWSBURYS,
Charleston, Va.
April 2. [37

Oldest known advertisement for Kanawha River packet.

Improvements on the Kanawha did a great deal to stimulate steamboat traffic. With the legislature of Virginia's continued appropriations, major problem areas to navigation such as the mouth of the Elk River, Johnsons, Tylers and Red House Shoals were improved. This along with the growing trade possibilities in the valley did much to encourage more steamboats to work the Kanawha.

During the last half of 1829 and the first half of 1830 commerce on the Kanawha was very active. River conditions were good and boats were arriving and departing Charleston with regularity.

The new steamer *Oliver H. Perry* arrived at Charleston on Thursday August 4, 1829 and departed for Cincinnati discharging her freight and passengers. The *Perry* was one of those steamboats that now made weekly stops at Charleston. The two other boats were the *Paul Pry* and the *Emigrant* sailing from Cincinnati and Louisville.

Again on January 16, 1830, the *Paul Pry, Oliver H. Perry* and the *Emigrant* were at Charleston where the *Western Register* stated: "Travelers will find these boats a safe, expeditious, and cheap conveyance; and will seldom be detained at this place more than three days."

Even the Charleston Hotel used the regularity of packet services as a part of their advertising in the *Kanawha Banner*... "Every facility will be offered to such persons as may call on him (the proprietor) to insure as speedy an embarkation on steamboats as practicable. There will be a small but comfortable steam packet engaged in transporting the mail from Charleston to Gallipolis, (the Chillicothe, Columbus and Northwest Mail) on the Ohio River which together with two other steamboats employed on this river will at almost all times afford to travelers the agreeable alternative of a speedy passage by water."

So important was steamboat travel that daily reports were made on river conditions and the arrival and departure of all the boats. The time it took to make a trip between two towns by a local steamboat was always a source of news for the papers. On March 26, 1830, the *Western Register* proclaimed "The steamer *Oliver H. Perry* arrived at this port on Sunday last in forty hours from Pittsburgh with a full cargo of freight and passengers."

The new mechanical marvel of the developing frontier soon spawned a boat building industry with steamboats being constructed at almost any location on the river. The Kanawha was no exception with steamboats being built at some unusual places. One example of this is the steamer *Olivia* that was built at Vintroux Landing, (near Red House) Virginia and then taken to Cincinnati to be completed in 1847. Built by Captain Isaac B. Parker and L. E. Vintroux to run in the Cincinnati-Kanawha River trade, the *Olivia* became the boat that a young Horace E. Bixby was to learn the river on. Bixby started out on the *Olivia* as her "mud clerk" (this was the person, usually with muddy feet and pant legs who stood at the end of the landing stage on the river bank and accounted for all on-coming and off-going freight) and gradually worked himself up to become her pilot. Bixby would later in his career "learn the river" to a young Samuel Clemens (Mark Twain) while working on the Mississippi River.

Between 1834 and 1857 there were eleven steamboats documented as being built on the Kanawha River according to the Merchant Steam Vessels of the United States, 1790-1868 (The Lytle-Holdercamper List). However there were several other boats built on the Kanawha but apparently never officially documented.

Among these boats was the *Texas* that was built at the mouth of Big Buffalo Creek in 1837 by the Summers brothers. After running for about a year she had an accident, was rebuilt and renamed the *Saline*.

In 1838 the steamer *Osceola* was built at Buffalo by Dr. Putney, William Atkeson and Samuel Summers.

The steamer *Herman* was built at Buffalo in 1847 for the Cincinnati-Kanawha River trade. Shortly after being built, the *Herman* was chartered by the U.S. Government and sent to Mexico with a cargo of supplies for the army. She never returned to the Kanawha.

The building of new steamboats was always of great interest to the public. In 1837, a company of men from Cincinnati built a large passenger steamboat for the Kanawha River trade. A man

THE BANNER.

CHARLESTON, SEPTEMBER 2, 1831.

THE Steamboat **EMIGRANT,** WILL ply regularly between Kanawha and Cincinnati, whenever the water will permit.—For freight or passage apply to JOHN LEWIS or JAMES HEWETT, Kanawha Salines; to JOHN F. FAURE, Charleston; to JAMES H. FRY at Coal's Mouth, or to the Captain on board. LEWIS, IRELAND & FRY.

Louisville 7th Dec 1832
Board Emigrant for Nashville

My dear Coleman,

As we leave this for Nashville this morning & it being somewhat uncertain when we will as high up as Charleston Kan— I seize the opportunity of writing a line or two by Mr. Nowman

I wish you would get my coat & send it by some of the Kanawha Boats to me— If you send it, put it in the direct charge of some Clerk that you can confide in & direct him to keep it untill he lands at the same port with the Emigrant & then deliver it to me for the old blue has some of the marks of the Molasses & salt Blls— Do not fail if a good chance offers—

I shall be a perfect Navigator when I see you again I have explored these mundane Shores— My fingers are so cold that I can scarcely write— Except with assurance of Regard from Cook

December 7, 1832 letter written on the steamboat *Emigrant* while landed at Louisville, Kentucky.
Coleman is Captain Nelson Coleman of Charleston, West Virginia.

Reprinted at right for ease of reading.

Louisville 7th Dec 1832
Boat Emigrant for Nashville

My dear Coleman,

As we leave this (port) for Nashville this morning & it being somewhat uncertain when we will (be) as high up as Charleston Kan— I seize the opportunity of writing a line or two by Mr. Nowman.

I wish you would get my coat & send it by some of the Kanawha Boats to me — If you send it, put it in the direct charge of some clerk that you can confide in & direct him to keep it until he lands at the same port with the Emigrant & then deliver it to me for the old blue has some of the marks of the molasses & salt barrels. Do not fail if a good chance offers—

I shall be a perfect navigator when I see you again. I have explored these mundane shores. My fingers are so cold that I can scarcely write(.) Except (accept) with assurance of regard(.) from

Cook

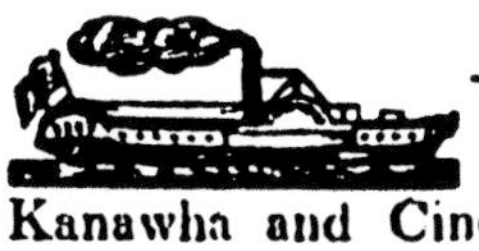

S. B. Tuckahoe

To Robert Wallace Dr.

1838							
Februa	15	To 4 Galls Whiskey	35		1	40	
		" 1 " Brandy			2	50	
		" 1 " Rum			2	50	6 40
March	6	" 1 Loaf Sugar	6¼	11		71	
		" 4 Galls Whiskey		37	1	50	
		" 4 " Gin		75	3	00	
		" 4 " F. Brandy		150	6	00	
		" 1 " Cog Ale			2	50	
		" 1½ " H. Gin			3	75	17 46
	12	" 72℔ Bro Sugar		8			5 76
	15	" 1 Galls Mad Wine			2	50	
		" 1 " Whiskey			1	00	
		" 1 " Gin			2	50	
		" 2 " Brandy		250	5	00	
		" 1 " Whiske		30	1	32	

living in the eastern part of Virginia, hearing about the new boat, wrote to the company offering them fifty dollars for the privilege of naming the boat. The offer was accepted and the *Tuckahoe* started her Kanawha River trade that fall.

The engines and machinery used on steamboats was often used on many different boats. To illustrate this practice consider the steamboat *Enterprise*, the first towboat on the Kanawha. She was built at Pittsburgh about 1830 and was commanded by Captain James Payne. The *Enterprise* was dismantled in 1835 and her engines and machinery were placed in the sidewheel *Hope* built at Pt. Pleasant in 1836.

The *Hope* was dismantled in 1841 and her machinery was used in building the *Jim* in 1843 at Red House. The *Jim* was taken to Mobile by Captain Alfred Brown who traded her for a sidewheel steamer named *Catawba*. The *Catawba* was brought back to run on the Kanawha but was soon sold to run on the Tennessee River.

Between 1840 and 1860 the number of steamboats operating on the Kanawha grew in number with their activities being a regular feature in the Charleston newspapers.

During March 1843 these arrivals and departures were announced: On the 11th, the *Thames* arrived from Nashville and the *Lawrence* left for Cincinnati. On the 12th, the *Spartan* arrived from Cincinnati and the *Lelia* from Parkersburg. The *Return* arrived from Pt. Pleasant on the 13th while the *Thames* left for the Wabash River.

During the first week of April, 1843, the *Lelia* made the fastest run between Charleston and Cincinnati to that time. She left Charleston at 10:30 a.m., Sunday the 2nd, arrived at Cincinnati at 9:30 a.m. on Monday the 3rd. She departed Cincinnati at 7:00 p.m. that evening, arriving at Charleston at 1:30 p.m. on Wednesday. This was not a direct run but did include regular wharflandings and business time. This three day, three hour trip was long the talk of Kanawha rivermen.

Cargo carried on the boats varied from heavy cargo and people to small personal packages. April 15, 1843, one of the larger and better packets on the Kanawha, the *Martha*, left Charleston with emigrants bound for the upper Mississippi River ports of St. Louis, Galena, Dubuque and intermediate points.

In May of the same year the package business on the Kanawha packets became so burdensome that the *Lelia* and *Lawrence* announced that they would carry no package for less than fifty cents. The reason for this new policy was that the articles they were requested to carry were available from local merchants at the same price or less as those in Cincinnati.

By the late 1850's larger, better built boats were running in regular trade on the Kanawha.

On August 2, 1859, the new steamer *Ellen Gray* arrived at Charleston on her maiden trip. Built at Cincinnati on a hull 150 feet long, 24 feet wide with a hold of 3 feet, the *Ellen Gray* became one of the most popular steamboats ever to navigate the Kanawha. Mrs. B. Z. Winter, a Charleston resident, was so fond of the boat that she wrote the following poem.

The Ellen Gray

On the broad Ohio's bosom
Where the sparkling sunbeams play,
Floats a barque of fairy model
Bonnie little *Ellen Gray.*

In her cabin all is pleasant,
Clean and tasteful, fair and neat;
Soft luxurious chairs invite you—
Carpets sink beneath your feet.

Everything for ease and comfort
On the *Ellen Gray* you'll find,
And her gallant Clerk and Captain,
Ever most obliging kind.

Don't forget this ye that travel;
Be your preference where it may.
There's no boat upon the waters
Like the bonnie *Ellen Gray.*

Many of the boats now running on the Kanawha would soon become involved in the conflict that was soon to engulf the entire nation. Among the boats that would be involved in the Civil War on the Great Kanawha River were the *Allen Collier, Julia Maffitt,* and *Kanawha Valley No. 2.*

SHIPPED

IN GOOD ORDER AND WELL CONDITIONED,

By William & Nat. Poyntz,

for account and risk of whom it may concern, on board the good Steam Boat *Lawrance* whereof is master for the present voyage now lying at the Port of Maysville, and bound for *Kanawha* the following articles, marked and numbered as below, which are to be delivered, without delay, in like good order, at the port of *Kanawha Saline* (the dangers of the river, fire and other unavoidable accidents only excepted,) unto Mr. C. G. Reynolds or to his assigns; he or they to pay freight for the said goods, at the rate of

In Witness Whereof, The Owner, Master or Clerk of said Boat has affirmed to 2 bills of lading, all of this tenor and date, one of which being accomplished, the other 1 to stand void. Dated at Maysville, the 24 day of Aug 1841

Marked
C. G. Reynolds

3 Bags Coffee 16 v
188

WVSA

In 1840 the *Elk* and the Steamer *Hope* were chartered to make an excursion to Pomeroy, Ohio where General William Henry Harrison was to make a political speech. The two boats were lashed together and carried a large house built of buckeye logs representing Ohio, the Buckeye State.

Regular Cincinnati Packet!

The new light draught steamer

ELK *Caffrey master,*

will run regularly between Kanawha and Cincinnati.-

Leave Charleston punctually at 9 o'clock every Thursday morning. Leave Cincinnati, every Saturday evening at 4 o'clock.

Passengers arriving at Charleston in the Eastern stage may rely upon taking the Elk at the hour above stated. [June 11, 1844.

Lewisburg Observer and *Lynchburg Virginian* copy to amount of $2 and charge this office.

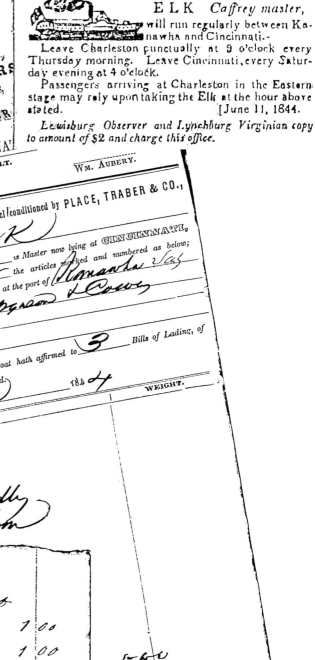

1844 receipt for wharfage fees to the Corporation of Charleston for the Steamer *Elk*.

Account book of the steamboat *Elk* setting forth crews wages in the upper half and receipts in the lower half. The names are a veritable "who's-who" of prominent pioneer Kanawha valley families.

Steam Boat Elk	Dr.	November 17	1844
To Amt due	N. Wells — captain	14.51⅓	
" " "	William Wylie — 1st Pilot	5.00	
" " "	A. F. Finney — 2d "	4.75	
" " "	Skelton Cox — 1st Engineer	5.35⅓	
" " "	William Wards — 2d "	6.83⅓	
" " "	J. H. Miller — Clerk	6.33⅓	
" " "	John Montague — Mate	3.33⅓	
" " "	Collins Soms — Steward	5.91⅓	
" " "	Henrietta Bowes — Chambermaid	6.80	
" " "	Nelson Bills — Fireman	2.00	
" " "	George Cabble "	1.50	
" " "	Larry Conway Deck Hand	3.50	
" " "	Henry Harmon " "	1.00	
" " "	J. Clark " "	5.00	
" " "	Hugh Anderson 2d Cook	.80	
" " "	John Lewis Cabin boy	.80	
" " "	Charles Ralston 1st Cook	2.33⅓	
		81.30	
" " "	Whittington for wood	12.03	
" " "	Broadwell & Co	25.40	
		118.73	

Cr.			
By Amt due from	Place & Soaler for on Salt		1.72
" " " "	Charles G. Reynolds		5.00
" " " "	William Tompkins		38.32½
" " " "	Lewis Ruffner		35.00
" " " "	F. Walker		10.00
" " " "	Joel Shrewsbury Sr		6.00
" " " "	Van B. Donnally		6.00
" " " "	Col A. Donnally		4.00
" " " "	John D Lewis		4.00
" " " "	H. Morris		11.94½
" " " "	M. Hansford		16.42½
" " " "	J. Downward		2.70
" " " "	Sundry Small accts		10.10½
" " " "	Jno. M. Clarkson		5.00
" " " "	Dr. S. Patrick		4.00
			159.22

Stage connections and acceptable lodging were very important to the success of both early Kanawha and Ohio River packets. The Cincinnati-Guyandotte packets were the first mail boats on the upper Ohio.

DAILY STAGES

ARE NOW RUNNING BETWEEN

Charleston and Guyandotte;

CONNECTING AT GUYANDOTTE WITH

THE FOLLOWING LINE OF FIRST CLASS

STEAM PACKETS:

FORMING A DAILY LINE TO CINCINNATI.

Sunday	Little Ben	Capt. Thacker	Up
	Majestic	" Bennett	Down
Monday	Brunette	" Irwin	Up
"	Cutter	" Collins	Down
Tuesday	Clipper	" Crooks	Up
"	Monongahela	" Stone	Down
Wedn'day	Majestic	" Bennett	Up
"	Hibernia	" Klinefelter	Down
Thursday	Cutter	" Collins	Up
"	Little Ben	" Thacker	Down
Friday	Monongahela	" Stone	Up
"	Brunette	" Irwin	Down
Saturday	Hibernia	" Klinefelter	Up
"	Clipper	" Crooks	Down

Passengers leave Cincinnati on the above boats every morning, arrive at Guyandotte next morning, and Charleston next evening, or in 35 hours.

Passengers leave Charleston every morning in superior four horse Post Coaches, arrive at Guyandotte same evening, and Cincinnati next morning, or in 24 hours.

☞ Passengers by this line have precedence in the Eastern Stage over all others.   WM. PETTES.
June 25, 1844—tf

KANAWHA AND CINCINNATI PACKET

The new, light-draught, and substantial steamer PLANET, RICHARD ROBERTSON Master, having been purchased expressly for the above trade, will commence her regular trips in due season; leaving Kanawha every Wednesday morning at 9 o'clock, A.M. and Cincinnati every Saturday at 12 o'clock, M.

The Planet's accommodations, for speed and comfort, will not be surpassed (if equalled) by any boat in the trade. Shippers and passengers may rely on her punctuality, and all business entrusted to my care will meet with every necessary attention—in return for which I only ask of my friends, and the public generally, a deserving share of their patronage.
October 22, 1845

VIRGINIA HOUSE,

KEPT BY

P. W. HALE & CO.
POINT PLEASANT, VA.

THIS is the nearest house to the steamboat landing, and has large and commodious rooms well ventilated. The proprietors have just opened the house for the reception of guests, and are determined that nothing on their part shall be omitted in endeavoring to make this house worthy of the patronage of the travelling community, as well as of the public generally. There is attached to the premises a stable, which will always be provided with an attentive hostler and plenty of provender.

There is a daily line of Stages running from this place eastward, by the way of the White Sulphur Springs; also a tri-weekly line to the west, by way of Chilicothe. Extra stages will always be in readiness to take passengers after the regular stages has started out.   P. W. HALE & CO.
Point Pleasant, Sept. 24. 1845

Office of the Clerk Dis: Court
Gallia County

Gallipolis, 22d Aug. 1859.

S. A. Miller, Esq:

Dear Sir: The amount of judgment in the case of Almer Bruce vs. Steamboat Salem, entered at the April Term A. D. 1859 is - - - - - *$500.00*
Amount of costs " *34.70*
Total - - *$534.70,*
with interest thereon from April 18. 1859.
Very Respectfully

James M. Campbell, Clerk D. C. G.
By J. L. Vance Deputy.

WVSA

The steamer Salem has gone to Cincinnati with the expectation of going in the
dock, and consequently may not be looked for on Thursday next. She will resume
her trips the next week, provided there is
water sufficient.

The Jane Franklin has laid up at Point
Pleasant repairing and painting for the
summer business, and will be in the trade
again as soon as the water will permit.

Yesterday the river was rising slowly

☞ The river is low, but still at a fair
steamboat stage. The Salem has made
her current weekly trip, with a fair freight
and passengers; the little Hurricane arrived on Tuesday after we had gone to
press; the Winifrede was at the wharf on
Friday, and the A. Wood is making her
semi-weekly trips to Gallipolis. We wish
them plenty of water and fair freights!

☞ The steamer Salem, on her last
trip from Cincinnati, took off the passengers and cargo of the steamer R. H. Lind-
sey, that was wrecked on the Ohio near
Greenupsburg, Ky. The L. plied as a
packet between Portsmouth and Pomeroy,
Ohio. She stove a hole in her bottom in
attempting to land, and was in a sinking
condition when the Salem came to her
aid.

Steamboat activity, principally the
steamer *Salem*, as reported in the
Kanawha Republican, June 6, 1855.

1840 agreement of unknown parties to build a Kanawha River steamboat to be named *Gen'l Bleucher*. Since no such named boat is known to exist, it can be assumed that the boat was not built or was given a different name if built.

Be it K___n That we the undersigned, being desirous to build a Steam Boat for the Kanawha river, bind and oblige ourselves, heirs &c to pay the several amts annexed to our names, w___ the Superintendant or managers of said boat when called for, or such a proportion of it as may be necessary to commence, carry on, and complete said boat, in such a manner as may be deemed most prudent, by said Superintend or managers, and it is a stipulated condition that the name of said boat shall be "Gen'l Bleucher" and that the construction, erection and completion of said boat shall be under the immediate controul of

and for the better purpose of satisfying the owners of said boat, they, or majority of them shall appoint three individuals among themselves, to whom the Captain or master of said boat shall render an a/c of the business of the Boat whenever they may require it, and any instructions from the said three individuals shall at all times be binding upon the Commanding officer of said boat in witness whereof we annex our names, this 16th day of Mch 1840

WVSA

Bills of Lading from the records of the steamboats *Levi Welch*, *Skipper* and *Kanawha Valley*.

— 23 —

FREIGHT   BOOK.

Trp No. _1_ From _Kanawha Salines_   To _Cincinnati January 25_ 1851

Shippers' Names.	Residence.	Consignees.	Destination.	Marks.	Description of Freight.	Weight.	Rate.	Amount.	Cash.	Charges.	Remarks.
John P Hale	Salines	John Lovell	Concord, Ky		50 Barrels Salt	28	14.00	14.00			
W.D. Shrewsbury	" "	T Arthur	" "		94 Barrels Salt	28	26.32	26.32			
T. Hoe	" "	T. Hoe	Cabbin Creek		1 Lot Mooring Plunder		5.00	5.00			
M. Kellogg	Charleston	Peter Neff	Cincinnati		3 Barrels Cannel Coal	25	75	75			
Sattis	" "	C Sattis	" "	on Board	8 Barrels Tallow	37½	3.00	3.00			
Martin Beck	" "	Sattis	Portsmouth		13 Ale Barrels Error		0.00	0.00			Balliot of Co.
Smith Washington	Salines	McVae & Co	Portsmouth		3 Large Boxes Tobacco	37½	1.12	1.12			Wharf Marks
					31 do Small	10	4 12½	4.12			
Jesse Watton	Mo Race	A McMullen	Cincinnati		1000 Feet Lumber	41		4.00			Charged
M. Carper	Walnut Grove	M Carper	"				4.00	4.00			
John F.											

Malden June 7 1857

M N P Coleman

To Steamboat AURILLA WOOD, Dr.

For Freight on _1 Bbl Flour_ _1 kg_   35   8.50   8.85

Recd payment

SHIPPED IN GOOD ORDER & WELL CONDITIONED, By BROOKS & BROTHER, On the good Steam Boat _Olivia_ now lying at Cincinnati, the articles marked and numbered as below, which are to be delivered in like good order and condition at the Port of _Kanawha Salines_ (the dangers of the River and unavoidable accidents excepted,) unto _C. Ingles_ or assigns, he or they paying freight at the rate of _Customary_

In Witness Whereof, the Owner, Master or Clerk of said Boat hath affirmed to three Bills of Lading, of this tenor and date, one of which being accomplished, the others to stand void.

Dated at CINCINNATI, this 15 day of _June_ 1850

MARKS.	ARTICLES.	WEIGHTS.
C. Ingles	Wood Shingles	

WVSA

IRLC

Str. "Virginia Home"

Designed and built for Kanawha River trades by Captain William F. Gregory after buying the hull from John Viney of Gallipolis, Ohio. Named for Captain Gregory's hometown, Richmond, Virginia, the *Virginia Home* was the first steamboat to reach the Kanawha Falls in 1858. Captain Gregory later wrote about the trip, "Col. Stockton offered $500 for the first boat to go to the Falls but he never paid me the reward; instead he gave me two barrels of flour, 1 bushel of meal, some venison hams and one ham of bear meat. His daughter gave me 6 chickens and a whole lot of preserves. During the war a good many boats went to the Falls, that being 1863 and 1864, during high water." The *Virginia Home* was lost when she overturned in a storm four miles below Cincinnati on May 21, 1860.

Steamer *Freestone*

Built in 1858 at Murraysville, Virginia. (West Virginia) and completed at Cincinnati, the *Freestone* operated with the *Virginia Home* and the *John Buck* in what was referred to as the "railroad" trade in the summer of 1859.

The "railroad" trade was carrying passengers and package freight between Parkersburg and Scott's Landing (Moore's Junction) on the Ohio River for the B & O and the Marietta and Cincinnati Railroads.

No records were located for the steamer *Wm. H. Langley* during the research for this book. However, noting that her captain was A. Donnally assures that she operated on the Kanawha.

Early Racing On The Kanawha River

Not all the residents of the Kanawha valley were sure that the steamboat was a permanent fixture on the river even twelve years after the *Andrew Donnally* had made her first landing at Charleston.

In 1833, Mr. Sutton Matthews made a wager of $500.00 with Captain N. B. Coleman that a canoe with six strong men could beat his steamboat, the *Daniel Webster*, in a race. The canoe was a long, slim and well proportioned "dugout", highly polished and varnished to lessen the friction of the water. It was manned by six young, athletic rowers eager to pit their power against that of a four-year-old steamboat. Public interest in the race was keen and betting ran high with between $5,000 and $8,000 changing hands on the outcome of the race. Everyone from the staid, sober-sided citizens to deckhands on the steamboat and salt packers at the furnaces were willing to back their choice with money.

On the day of the race, the banks of the Kanawha were lined with people to witness the outcome. It turned out to be a short but sweet race for the *Daniel Webster* and her supporters. As the steamer wheels turned, waves were created that upset the canoe giving the rowers an unexpected and involuntary bath, as well as the defeat. Accounts of the race were carried in many newspapers of the time.

The Salt Well And The Harvard Professor

In 1843, while drilling for salt, the well went deep enough that when the drill bit went into the brine it brought up gas as well. The gas pressure made the salt water a fountain 150 feet high. Dr. John P. Hale, noted Kanawha Valley historian, relates the following story concerning this incident in G.W. Atkinson's 1876 History of Kanawha County: "While this well was blowing it was the custom of the (Kanawha Turnpike) stage drivers, as they passed down by it to stop and let their passengers take a look at the novel and wonderful display.

On one occasion, a professor from Harvard College was one of the stage passengers, and being a man of an investigating and experimenting turn of mind, he went as near the well as he could get for the gas and spray of the falling waters, and lighted a match to see if the gas would burn. Instantly the whole atmosphere was ablaze, the professor's hair and eyebrows singed and his clothes a-fire. The well-frame and engine-house also took fire, and were much damaged. The Professor, who had jumped into the river to save himself from the fire, crawled out, and back to the stage as best he could, and went to Charleston, where he took to bed, and sent for a doctor to dress his burns. The well owner told his man to go to Charleston and have the culprit arrested for destroying his property, "unless" he said, you find that the fellow is a natural d__d fool, and didn't know any better. The Professor from Harvard, considering the alternatives, admitted that he was a natural d__d fool, and the matter ended".

1850 Map of Charleston

In 1850 the State of Virginia sponsored a project that was to connect the James River and Kanawha Canal with the Ohio River.

Although never built, the Covington & Ohio Railroad was surveyed by C. B. Shaw, the principal engineer for the Virginia Board of Public Works, and his maps were later utilized by the C & O Railroad in the 1870's. It is believed to be the oldest known map of Charleston and this the first printing.

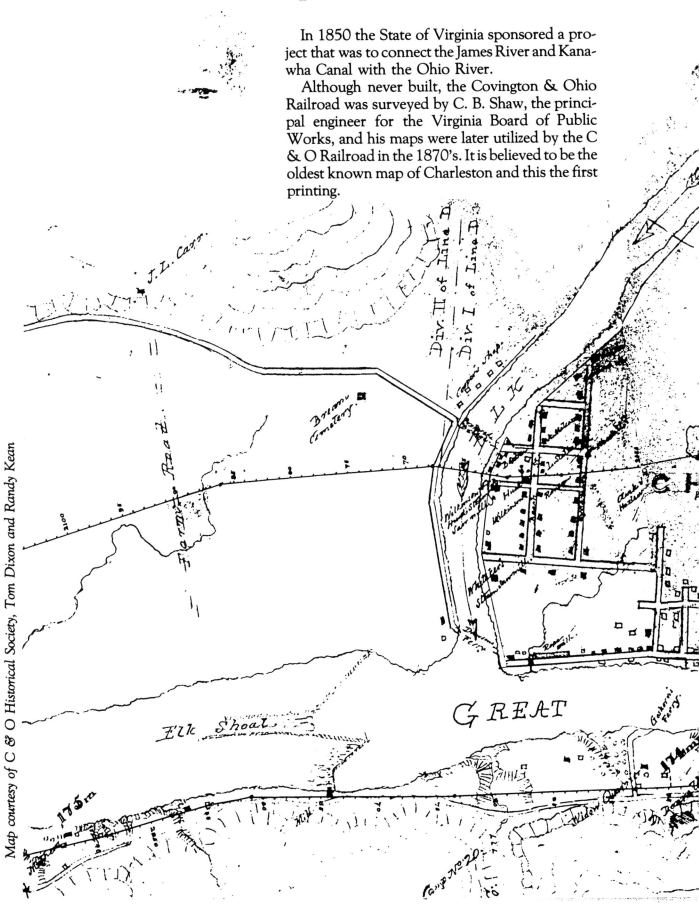

Map courtesy of C & O Historical Society, Tom Dixon and Randy Kean

Beginning at top center note the prominent location of the gallows—an indication of justice for the time.

Most of the east end of the city was farmland and some swampy areas.

At the lower right along the river are listings of early settlers.

At the bottom center is the steamboat landing and Wilson's Ferry (at the end of Capitol Street) and the Cooper Shop across the river.

Just downstream, the Court House (corner of Boulevard and Court Street) and across the river, Goshorns Ferry.

Near the mouth of the Elk River, there is Davidson's Ferry, with the Rope Mill about where the Blue Cross Building is today.

Up the Elk River is the notation - Proposed Bridge. Later built as a wire suspension bridge which was destroyed during the Civil War.

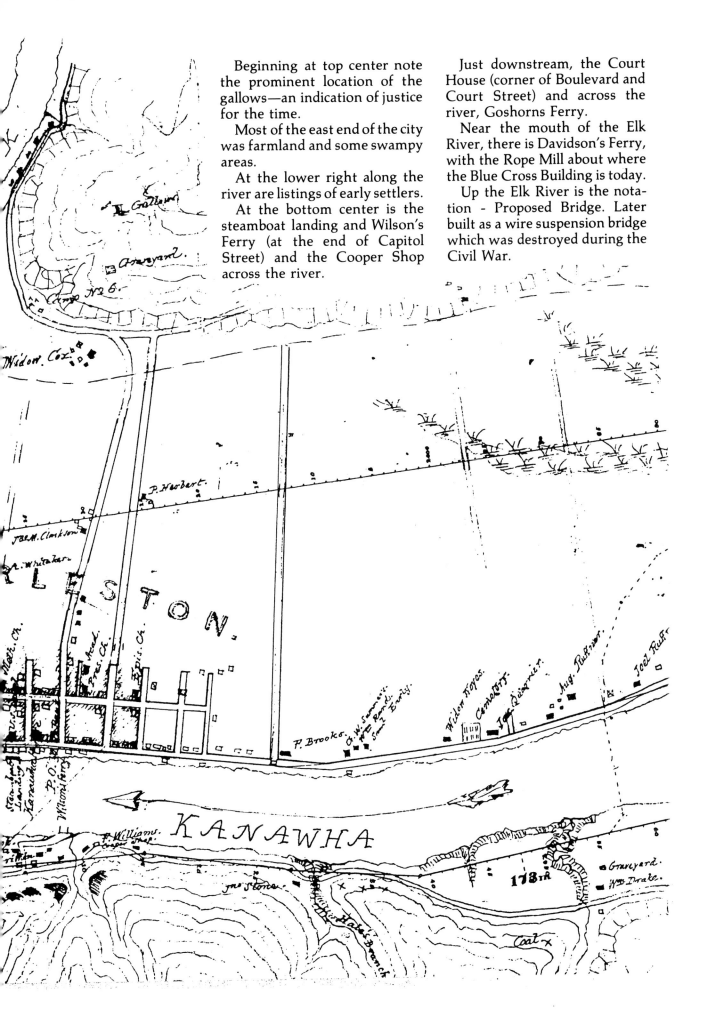

As all to often happens with historic events, they become muddied with time and their re-telling. This is the case of stories relating to bells that once belonged to Kanawha River steamboats.

Kanawha River Steamboats and Steamboat Bells

—Bell from the steamer *Robert Thompson*—

The Str. *Robert Thompson* was the first steamboat to ascend the Kanawha River as far as the Red House Shoals in 1819. Unable to pass the shoals after repeated tries, she steamed back down to Kanawha never to sail upon the river again.

For years there have been stories that the bell from the *Robert Thompson* hung in the yard of J.A. Noffsinger's home about a mile below Red House. Mr. Noffsinger's father Edward had hung it there after buying it from Frank Ruffner in 1874. How and when the bell came into Ruffner's possession is not known.

In his 1983 book, *History of Red House*, author Charles Ray Harper relates how on July 11, 1966 he visited the residence of Mr. and Mrs. L.R. Burkett on U.S. Route 35 opposite the New York Central Railroad yards to inquire about the story he had read concerning a steamboat bell. Mrs. Burkett took him around to the back of her house and showed him a bell hanging at the door of an outbuilding. As she swung the clapper to ring the bell, a wasp stung her hand.

It seems that this bell had been passed down through Mrs. Burkett's family (Noffsinger) for many generations. She then told Mr. Harper that the bell had been acquired by her grandfather from the Ruffner farm. The bell supposedly came off the first steamboat to come up the Kanawha River. The bell contained no names or dates.

It is difficult to understand why the owners of the *Robert Thompson* would sell or give the boat's bell to the Ruffners or anyone else for that matter. The *Thompson* continued to operate on the Ohio and other rivers for a number of years after trying to reach Charleston. (*See Chapter 2*).

—Bell from the steamer *Lelia*—

Today the bell from the steamboat *Lelia* is on display at the Cultural Center, Capitol Complex in Charleston. A card attached to the bell provides this information: "This bell was the first bell on the Kanawha River, was cast in 1825, brought to the Kanawha River in 1827 by the steamer *Lelia*, which was the first to carry a bell. The *Lelia* wrecked in 1837 and Kanawha County used the bell on the courthouse for 47 years. In 1897 it was presented to the historical department for the museum."

This bell had been cast by John Wilbank of Philadelphia.

As can be seen, the stories of the bells from the *Robert Thompson* and the *Lelia* contradict each other in dates or times. The mysteries of history cannot always be solved with the information available.

WVSA

—Bell from the steamer *Blue Ridge*—

In Janaury 1848, after leaving Gallipolis, Ohio on her way to Cincinnati, the steamer *Blue Ridge* exploded her boilers in the vicinity of Racoon Island. The *Blue Ridge* was a regular Kanawha River and Cincinnati side-wheeler and although there are stories that she blew up on the Kanawha River below Red House, a letter in the possession of Mrs. John Rutherford of Charleston, W. Va. written by her great uncle W. B. Koontz from Guyandotte, Virginia on January 10, 1848 relates his personal account of the accident on the Ohio River.

Mr. Koontz had written the letter to his mother explaining that he had been aboard the *Blue Ridge* when she exploded and that he was all right and that she was not to worry. After the explosion, the cabin had drifted downstream about four miles before a yawl had rescued Mr. Koontz, James Ruffner of Kanawha, Major Jubal Early of the army of Mexico and others.

This Major Jubal Early, who was later to gain fame as a Confederate General in the Civil War, had been on leave to visit his father on a farm near the town of present-day Buffalo, W. Va. He had contracted rheumatism in Mexico and was recuperating at home.

At the time of the explosion, half of Major Early's stateroom was carried away and pieces of boiler-iron "protruded through the floor cutting and burning his feet." He suffered no other ill effect of the accident, although between 11 and 15 lives were lost.

Another person involved in the explosion was Captain William Penn Wright, who was a member of the boat's crew. At the time of the explosion, Captain Wright had been blown overboard, swam ashore and then walked through a fresh-fallen one inch snow some forty miles back up the Kanawha Valley to his home at Red House.

This Kanawha River Wright family has produced 36 licensed masters, pilots and engineers. Harold Bell Wright, a grandson of William Penn Wright was to save the lives of 21 of the passengers and crew of the steamer *Kanawha* in 1916. (*See Chapter 4*).

Today the bell of the *Blue Ridge* hangs on the porch of the Putnam County Courthouse. Putnam County was formed in the State of Virginia in 1848, the same year as the *Blue Ridge* explosion.

LIEUTENANT-GENERAL JUBAL A. EARLY, C. S. A.
FROM A PHOTOGRAPH.

Steamer *Blue Ridge* Bell

One of the finest artifacts of the history of steamboating on the Great Kanawha is the bell off the *Blue Ridge* hanging today at the Putnam County Court House.

After the *Blue Ridge* blew up in the Ohio River in 1848 her bell was recovered and brought to Winfield, Virginia (W.Va.). In 1850 a courthouse was built for Putnam County at Winfield and the splendid bell of the *Blue Ridge* was installed in the steeple.

About 1900 a fierce windstorm destroyed the old courthouse and apparently cracked the bell. When the building was reconstructed a new bell was placed in the steeple, however for sentimental reasons the old *Blue Ridge* bell was retained and mounted on the ceiling of the porch directly over the front steps. It has remained there for 90 years in clear view although few living today know or would appreciate its significance.

Molded into the bell are *Buckeye Foundry - Cincinnati Ohio 1845.*

Photo by R. A. Andre

Struggle, Steam and Gunsmoke

Built in 1855 at Cincinnati, the steamer *Moses McLellan* ran in the Cincinnati-Memphis trade before the war. Sold to the Upper Mississippi River in 1862 to run as a LaCrosse & St. Paul Railroad Packet. She was rebuilt and named *City of St. Paul* in 1866.

Captain William F. Gregory was seeing the Great Kanawha River as he had never seen it before. As he stood in the pilothouse of the big sidewheel steamer *Moses McLellan* with her master, Captain William Knight, the river seemed smaller than it ever had.

The *McLellan*, about 220 feet long, was the largest boat ever to run on the Great Kanawha. She had departed Gallipolis, Ohio loaded with over a thousand tons of supplies for the Federal troops encamped at Camp Piatt, 10 miles above Charleston.

In 1861, it wasn't just his steamers size and the conditions of the river that concerned Captain Knight, but it was the war that now raged in the valley and the nation as well.

After arriving at Camp Piatt and quickly unloading his cargo, Captain Knight ordered Gregory to turn the boat downstream and return to Gallipolis. However, turning the *McLellan* around in this narrow stretch of river proved to be impossible. Captain Gregory began to back the big steamer downstream. After backing about 12 miles, Gregory finally found a section of river wide enough to turn the *McLellan* and proceeded on to Gallipolis.

At the outbreak of the Civil War, the Kanawha River became an area of interest for both the Union and Confederates. The James River-Kanawha River route to the Ohio River valley and its strategic importance was not overlooked by either side. In addition, the vast salt works represented quite a prize for both armies.

Five days after the Civil War had started, Virginia seceded from the Union and began to move troops into the Kanawha Valley.

UP-HILL WORK.

Ohio to drive all Rebel troops and supporters out of the valley. In July, he deployed some of his troops along an overland route up the river while the main body of his troops were moving upstream aboard a flotilla of 12 steamboats including the *Economy, Mary Cook, Matamoras, Silver Lake No. 2,* and *Fanny McBurnie* led by the flagship *Eunice*. This flotilla was commanded by

BRIGADIER-GENERAL HENRY A. WISE, C. S. A.,
EX-GOVERNOR OF VIRGINIA.

Confederate Brigadier General Henry A. Wise and a small force of men consisting primarily of the Richmond Light Infantry Blues, the Pig Run Invincibles and two cavalry units arrived at Charleston on June 25, 1861 to secure the valley for the Confederate States.

In the meantime, Federal Brigadier General Jacob D. Cox was massing troops at Gallipolis,

MAJOR-GENERAL JACOB D. COX. FROM A PHOTOGRAPH.

Our first day's sail was thirteen miles up the river, and it was the very romance of campaigning. I took my station on top of the pilot-house of the leading boat, so that I might see over the banks of the stream and across the bottom-lands which bounded the valley. The afternoon was a lovely one. Summer clouds lazily drifted across the sky, the boats were dressed in their colors, and swarmed with men as a hive with bees. The bands played national tunes, and as we passed the houses of Union citizens, the inmates would wave their handkerchiefs to us and were answered by cheers from the troops. The scenery was picturesque, the gently winding river making beautiful reaches that open new scenes upon us at every turn.

Battles and Generals of the Civil War
—Gen. Jacob D. Cox

Original drawing done expressly for this book
by Dalton S. Moore.

Captain John McLure. As a result of the success of this operation, Captain McLure was later promoted to Commodore of the Kanawha U.S. Fleet.

Travel on the Kanawha during late June and early July could be very slow and as the flotilla proceeded, the steamboats would sometimes have to land, allow the troops to unload, and continue with caution to get over some of the shoals and bars. After clearing the obstacle, the troops would re-board and the boat would resume their journey.

After a small skirmish at the mouth of the Pocatalico River, the Union forces were engaged by a concentration of Confederates on July 17 at the mouth of Scary Creek just below St. Albans. Although this encounter lasted all day neither side won a decisive victory. General Wise, however, claimed "a glorious repulse of the enemy, if not a decided victory." After this action, Wise began moving his troops up the Kanawha and out of Charleston toward Gauley Bridge fearing entrapment.

In late July during this Confederate withdrawal, the small steamboat *Julia Maffitt* with a flatboat in tow, was loaded with supplies and about 700 Rebel soldiers, many of whom were the Kanawha Riflemen, for movement up the river. The *Maffitt* had been built at Cincinnati in 1860 for the Charleston-Cannelton trade and was owned and operated by Southern sympathizers. Carrying the Rebel troops and supplies was more than just 'another job' for the *Maffitt's* crew.

As the boat was steaming upstream, Union troops were observed moving toward the river down the north bank. (This would be just about where Dunbar is located today.) Turning downstream to escape the enemy, the *Maffitt's* lookout reported sighting another Union force moving up the valley. At this point, pilot Phil Doddridge turned the boat's bow toward the south shore, rang the engine room for slow ahead and buried the *Maffitt's* nose in the muddy bank.

As the Confederate troops scrambled to safety under fire from the Union soldiers the following action occurred as reported in the *Cincinnati Commercial*, under the heading of *Further news from the Kanawha Expedition* "....and Captain Carter, of the Cleveland Artillery, fired one shot into the Rebel steamer *Julia Maffitt*, which caused her boilers to explode, and she burned to the water's edge."

The end for the *Julia Maffitt* had come at the hands of the enemy but just three months earlier, the *Kanawha Valley No. 2* had been lost to Confederate forces in confusion that often occurs in war.

boat was hailed but Captain Farley refused to land and continued on upstream. In response to his failure to stop, some of the troops fired at the boat, riddling it with holes and killing one of the passengers. When the *Kanawha Valley No. 2* landed at Cannelton, and the baggage was being unloaded, there was a commotion about the incident. General Wise ordered her taken across the river and burned at what is now Montgomery. For years after the war, the charred hull could be observed during periods of low water.

Captain S.C. Farley was hired to move the baggage of the 22nd Kanawha Confederates from Charleston upstream to Cannelton, then head of navigation, on his steamer *Kanawha Valley No. 2.* As the steamer passed the men of the 22nd marching along the riverbank toward Cannelton, the

Throughout the war, steamboats were used by both sides as the valley was controlled by first one side and then the other. Some of the boats used were the *Undine, Florence, Reliance, Horizon* and *Izetta*. On September 25, 1861, a war correspondent for the *Cincinnati Times* reports leaving Camp Enyart on the Kanawha for Cincinnati aboard the steamer *Capitola*. The article states that 1,000 Union troops were moving up the banks of the river to rid the area between Camp Enyart and Gauley Bridge of "Secesh" cavalry.

The *Capitola* had been built at Wheeling the year before and spent most of the Civil War chartered to the U.S. Army. After the war she ran in the Nashville-Louisville trade.

The use of steamboats on the Kanawha during the war depended on the need of the armies. This is vividly illustrated in the recollection of Captain William E. Bahlmann of the 22nd Virginia Infantry, Confederate States of America.

After being wounded and captured, Captain Bahlmann was being moved down the Kanawha to the Union hospital at Gallipolis, Ohio. His account starts after reaching the Falls of the Kanawha: "Most of the party were put on a steamboat but through some oversight Captain Thompson and I were sent to Cannelton, now Montgomery. At Cannelton I found Steve Riggs. He invited us to the house of his father-in-law, Captain Farley, an old river man. We had with us two young Federals, wounded at Lewisburg. I hinted to Mr. Riggs to invite these two men in. After we reached the ladies, they dressed the wounds of Thompson and of me and I told them to dress the wounds of the two Federals which they did. I was trying to make fair weather for them.

We all four took dinner with the Farleys. Mr. Riggs gave me a $5 bill. That afternoon a steamboat came and carried us down to Charleston and we were placed in a hospital where we stayed 11 days.... From Charleston we were sent by boat to Gallipolis, Ohio where there was a regular military hospital. We reached Gallipolis somewhat early in the morning. I walked from the river with the officer of the guard while the others rode in an ambulance."

As the war continued, other steamboats were to experience the perils of operating on the Kanawha.

On March 29, 1863, the steamer *Victor No. 2*, under the command of Captain Fred Ford of Gallipolis, Ohio nearly added its name to the lists of casualties of the Kanawha. While proceeding downstream with U.S. Paymaster B.R. Cowen on board with a large amount of funds in his possession, the *Victor No. 2* was hailed by an individual who was apparently alone near Halls Landing. Captain Ford ordered the pilot to make the landing and pick up the passenger. Unknown to Cap-

tain Ford, laying in hiding was a force of Confederates who revealed themselves as the boat neared the shore and began firing. The *Victor No. 2* was immediately backed away from the shore while being pelted by lead balls. She was able to move beyond the range of the rifle fire but not before being thoroughly riddled. Captain Ford continued on to Point Pleasant, Virginia where he informed the Union commander, Captain Carter, of the presence of rebel troops. Captain Carter did not see fit to prepare any defenses for the town and was taken by surprise the following day by General Albert G. Jenkins.

As late as February 1864 travel on the Kanawha was not always safe for the Union soldiers. Captain Charles Regnier of the steamboat *B. C. Levi*, had just finished loading his boat with lumber at Point Pleasant on February 1, when he was ordered back to Gallipolis from where he had just come. Here he spent the night and most of the next day before returning to Point Pleasant to pick up Union General Eliakim P. Scammon. Arriving about dark, the General wished to proceed up the Kanawha to Charleston and request Captain Regnier to make the run that night. Because of high winds and stormy conditions, Captain Regnier informed the General that it was too dark and stormy to go beyond Red House Shoals. The *Levi* would have to pass the shoals by a dug chute and this would be extremely hazardous at night without enough light to see the walls. The captain explained that he could leave at 1 or 2 o'clock and still reach Charleston by morning. This did not suit General Scammon and he ordered the trip to begin at once.

Against the advice of the captain and his assistant quartermaster, Captain G.J. Stealey, the General insisted and the boat pulled out into the river at 7 o'clock and headed upstream. Although the night was dark and many of the landmarks hidden from the pilots' view, the boat arrived below the shoals at a little past 1:00 a.m. The captain then went to his cabin to retire where he found the General pacing back and forth and very disturbed by the delay. He was informed that the boat would continue upstream as soon as enough light permitted and that the pilot was to be called at 2:30. However, when the pilot got to the pilothouse he decided that it was still too dark to proceed safely.

At about this same time a unit of the 16th Virginia Cavalry, Confederate States of America under the command of Major James H. Nounnan arrived at Winfield and saw the boat laying near the opposite shore. A small boat was procured and Lieutenant E. G. Vertegans with twelve men jammed into the boat, silently stole across the river and boarded the B.C. Levi. After overpowering the crew and passengers, the Levi was run across to the Winfield side of the river where it remained until late the next morning. A large amount of the cargo of medical supplies and twenty horses were removed from the boat. She was then run down to the mouth of Hurricane Creek and landed about a half a mile below at Vintroux Landing. Here General Scammon, Captain William G. Pinckard, Lieutenants Frank Millward and William C. Lyons along with twenty-five non-commissioned officers and men were taken ashore. The crew and other passengers were ordered off the boat and the rebels put her to the torch with a loss of an estimated $100,000 worth of medicines and munitions. All of the Union privates and non-commissioned officers except one were paroled by their captors. General Scammon, Captain Pinckard, Lieutenants Millward and Lyons and Sergeant Thomas McCormick were taken to Logan Court House and then to Richmond.

The news of the capture was soon known and Union General Alfred N. Duffie sent Colonel Hayes with one hundred men in pursuit of the rebels. The chase lasted five days but the rebels eluded the Federals at every turn.

While the flames of war burned their brightest, some steamboat owners tried to operate as often as conditions permitted. Among these were the Allen Collier, Annie Laurie, Victor, Victor No. 3, T.J. Pickett and Kanawha Belle (1st). Sometimes operating during this period had its risks. The Victor was attached by a deputy U.S. Marshall in April 1862 for operating on the Kanawha without a U.S. license. While on September 27, 1862 the Allen Collier along with the steamer Belfast went to Augusta, Kentucky to act as gunboat when Morgan's Raiders invaded the town. However, upon learning that Morgan's troops had howitzers, the two steamers turned tail and left the scene.

When the *Silver Lake No. 2* came to Charleston in May, 1863, *The Kanawha Republican* wrote: "There came up the Kanawha, on Saturday last to our place, a formidable looking craft, clad in iron mail. Her guns, we should think, would do admirable execution against an enemy, at a pretty long distance. Capt. Rodgers, his officers and men, by their gentlemanly department and fighting spirit, have won the highest regard of our people."

The *Silver Lake No. 2* was built at Wellsville, Ohio in 1861 and sold to the U.S. Army. Her name was changed to *Marion* in 1865 and a year later she sank in Montana.

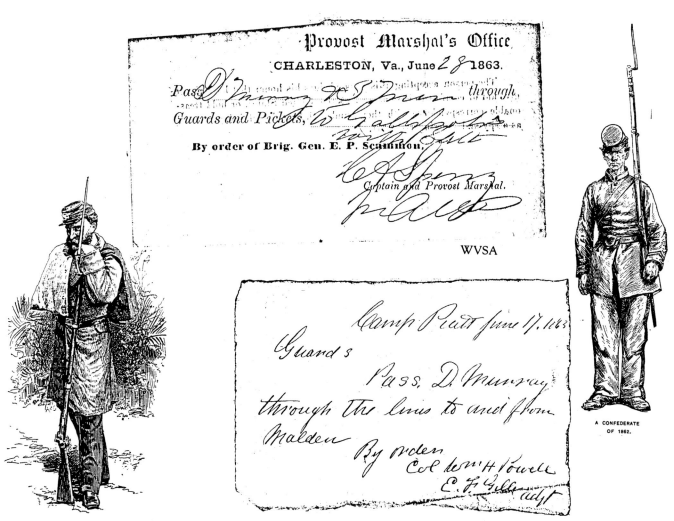

A CONFEDERATE OF 1862.

Report and Findings of the Court
Martial of Captain George W. Cox
of the steamboat *Victress*.

Headquarters 3d Division, Dep't W. Va.,

CHARLESTON, WEST VA., APRIL 29th, 1864.

GENERAL ORDERS.

No. 15.

I. Before a Military Commission, which convened at Charleston, West Va., on the 15th day of April, 1864, pursuant to Special Order No. 71, from these Headquarters, and of which Captain W. H. ZIMMERMAN, 23d Regt. Ohio Vol. Infantry, is President, were arraigned and tried:

1. Captain *Geo W. Cox*, of the steamer Victress:

CHARGE—"*Conduct highly prejudicial to the interest of the Government, endangering thereby the lives of its officers and soldiers, and rendering it's property liable to capture by the enemy.*"

Specification—In this, that Captain Geo. W. Cox, of the steamer Victress, a vessel then in service of the United States, did, on or about the night of the eighteenth of March, 1864, land and tie up the said steamer, some two miles and a half above Red House, a dangerous point on the Kanawha, and leaving the vessel at the mercy of the enemy, crossed over the river to Winfield, on a visit to his wife, and this was done in the face of the recent capture of Gen. Scammon and other officers, and the burning of the steamer B. C. Levi, and notwithstanding the best efforts of officers on board to prevent delay, and when ordered to put the boat, said steamer Victress, under way, the acting Captain refused to obey, saying that Captain Cox, on leaving the vessel, had ordered that she should not set out before four o'clock in the morning. The night was fine and clear, and the wind entirely lulled after ten o'clock.

To which charges and specifications the accused pleaded "Not Guilty."

FINDING—The Commission having maturely considered the evidence adduced, find the accused, Geo. W. Cox, Captain of the steamer Victress, as follows:

Of the Specification, (except in leaving the boat, and failing to run the schute after the wind lulled,) Not Guilty.
Of the Charge, Not Guilty.

SENTENCE.

And the Commission do therefore sentence him, the said Captain Geo. W. Cox, of the steamer Victress, "That he be not employed again in the Government service, and that he be not allowed to run a steamboat on the Kanawha river.

The evidence in this case does not warrant the finding. The whole proceedings are disapproved, and Captain Geo. W. Cox is released from his bonds.

WVSA

W. B. SMITH & Co., Stationers, Cincinnati.

SHIPPED,

IN GOOD ORDER AND WELL CONDITIONED, BY

F. WALKER & CO.

Commission Merchants,

Kanawha Salines, Va.

F. WALKER & CO.
COMMISSION AND FORWARDING
MERCHANTS,
AND DEALERS IN
SALT, DRY GOODS,
GROCERIES, IRON NAILS,
And Country Produce Generally.
Also, a general assortment of
READY MADE CLOTHING, ALWAYS ON HAND.

On board the good....Steam....Boat *Kana Valley No 2* whereof *Wallou*

is Master, now lying at KANAWHA SALINES, and bound for *Cincinnatti* the articles marked

and numbered as below, which are to be delivered without delay, in like good order at said Port, (the dangers of the River Fire and unavoidable accidents

excepted,) unto *C. Bodman* or assigns, he or they to pay freight at the rate of

In Witness Whereof, The Owner, Master or Clerk of said Boat hath affirmed to ..*1*. Bills of Lading, of this tenor and date, one of which

being accomplished, the others to stand void.

Dated at Kanawha Salines, this........*7*.....day of....*Oct*......186*0*

MARKS	ARTICLES.	WEIGHT.
C Bodman	1 Box Tobacco	
Cin	1 B...	

REGULAR CINCINNATI, MAYSVILLE, PORTSMOUTH, BIG SANDY, GALLIPOLIS & KANAWHA PA...

Capt. S. C. FARLEY.   H. R. McGUIRE Clerk.

To Steamer ALLEN COLLIER

MARKS	TO FREIGHT ON	
Due Samuel Turner	One Dollar & Sixty Seven	
Cents		

January... 1861

Steamer Julia Maffitt
Jos Wallon Clk.   Agent

Regular Gallipolis and Charleston Light-Draught Passenger Packet.

A. W. GARNER, Commander.   J Christie

M Capt Coleman   Jany 29th   1859

To Steamer VICTOR, Dr.

In no case whatever, will the Boat be responsible for damage to freight after it leaves the grade.

MARKS.	To Freight on		
	5 Sacks Bran		50
	Chgs	460	510

Payment.   W. S. Swayze Clerk.

THOS. WINTERS, Clerk.

Tribune Print.

Steamer *Annie Laurie* at Buffalo, W. Va. Photograph taken by Dr. C. M. Pitrat.

Captain Fred A. Laidley, who later formed the Louisville & Cincinnati Packet Co., took the *Annie Laurie* to Nashville and back for the U.S. Army in October 1864.

After the war she continued to operate on the Charleston-Cincinnati trade until she sank in the Kanawha in June 1869. She was raised, taken to Malden, W. Va. and dismantled.

NOTICE!
To Stockholders of S. B. Annie Laurie.

THE STOCKHOLDERS of the Steamboat Annie Laurie and the public generally, are hereby notified that I have this day sold my entire interest in the Steamboat Annie Laurie to John Slack, Jr., and will not be responsible for any accident that may happen her, or any debt she may contract. J. D. WHITE.
Charleston, Sept. 8, '64.
nov9-4w.

Steamer *Kanawha Belle* at Buffalo, W. Va. on the Kanawha River by Dr. C. M. Pitrat. This is the first *Kanawha Belle* built at Cincinnati in 1865 for the Charleston-Gallipolis trade. She appears to be stuck in this view with two men with sounding poles on the forecastle while the passengers watch.

In 1867 she was tied up at Maysville and was later dismantled. .

Steamboat advertisements appearing in the November 16, 1865 issue of the *West Virginia Journal* illustrates the competitive nature of the river trades on the Kanawha after the Civil War.

The *T. J. Pickett* along with the *Market Boy* worked for the Union Coal and Oil Company of Cannelton, W. Va. carrying crude oil in barrels from Cannelton to the refinery at Maysville during and after the Civil War.

In November 1865, the *T. J. Pickett* transported a group of New York investors interested in oil properties up the Kanawha to view possible investment sites.

Advertisements appearing in the 1865 *West Virginia Journal* for the developing packet trade after the Civil War.

Note also the proclamation of amnesty by the Governor for Confederate soldiers and supporters such as Isab Early (father of Rebel General, Jubal) in Putnam County.

Early Kanawha River Steamboat Photography—

The photographs appearing in this book of the steamers *Annie Laurie*, *Kanawha Belle* (1st), *R. W. Skillinger*, *Clara Scott*, *Active* and *Mount Clare* were either taken by or presume to have been taken by Dr. Claudius M. Pitrat of Buffalo, W. Va.

Born in Lyon, France on April 5, 1811, Pitrat became a medical student and based on his high standing during his schooling was appointed Surgeon in the French army.

He came to this country in the fall of 1839, settling at Buffalo on the Kanawha River.

Dr. Pitrat was not only a physician but an accomplished photographer, violinist and the Buffalo postmaster.

Dr. Pitrat died on Christmas day in 1891, four days after his wife had died. Their remains were carried to Gallipolis, Ohio aboard the steamer *Calribell* to be buried at Mound Hill.

With the end of hostilities, travel and commerce increased as the valley inhabitants interests returned to pre-war concerns.

Packetboat River

Charleston Riverfront, 1902 Steamer *Greenwood* landed at wharfboat with Steamer *Evergreen* along side. The *Cricket* was running in the Charleston-Montgomery trade. Captain Jesse P. Hughes Photo.

In 1929 Henry Holt and Company published a book by Charleston native Garnett Laidlaw Eskew titled *The Pageant of the Packets*. In Chapter I, author Eskew relates his early experiences with steamboats and the Charleston riverfront:

"Our levee was a fascinating place. It wasn't far from home either. You had only to walk a few hundred feet down Laidley Street; cut across State Street and Union School yard; slide quickly through my great Uncle Jim Brown's orchard and under the gnarled elms that bordered his driveway; proceed out Alderson Street to Front Street. And there you were. Front Street runs along on the top of the bluffs, and standing there, you could look down on the levee—a stone-and-gravel-paved causeway at the foot of which Donally's wharfboat lay in close to bank, stationary but floating, tethered to the bank so that it would rise and fall with the river. A hugh stage plank led from the bank to the wharfboat's great entrance, and over the stage plank all day long there came and went a motley procession of vehicles—drays and produce wagons and delivery carts, ice wagons and lumbering "floats."

And tied at the wharfboat, or a few hundred feet away, were nearly always a number of steamboats. The roustabouts, when the boat was loading or unloading, would keep up a continual movement on and off the decks. There were always a number of passengers in those days as well as a vast amount of miscellaneous freight."

Eskew then paints a vivid word picture of the steamboats regularly seen at the landing; the *Lizzie Bay, Kanawha, Henry M. Stanley, Tacoma, Greenwood, Greenland, Evergreen* and *Greendale*. These packets were carrying on the trades that had been established and developed by the Kanawha River's earliest packets.

In 1824 the little steamer *Fairy Queen* ran regular trips for some time in the Charleston and Cincinnati trade. She was followed in this trade by the *Paul Pry* who made regular trips for two years.

Although the number of packets on the Kanawha continued to increase prior to the Civil War, it was not until 1864 that the first regular packet with the quaint name of *Here's Your Mule* began operations above Charleston. The following year H.W. Goodwin established the first wharfboat at Charleston.

The importance of the steamboats to the economic and social life in the valley can best be illustrated by the newspaper articles as well as advertisements of the period.

In 1858 the General Assembly of Virginia established the Kanawha Board to administer the Kanawha River navigation and collect tolls on items shipped. After the Civil War, the new State of West Virginia continued to operate the Kanawha Board performing the same functions as its predecessor.

The secretary of the Kanawha Board in 1878 reported that "as nearly as can be gathered from the collector's reports of actual collections, the exports from the valley during the present year (1878) up to date; that is during eleven months:"

Coal, in tons of 2,000 pounds . . .	222,642
Salt, in bushels	125,000
Lumber in feet, B.M.	1,128,500
Staves	3,671,000
Railroad ties	16,800
Tan-bark, in cords	1,648
Hoop-poles	20,000
Miscellaneous tolls paid by packets	$1,484.26

"Of the miscellaneous tolls paid by packets a part should be for salt with which they freight down the river; part is for other exports, and a large part for imports. The actual commerce is greater than is indicated by the foregoing statistics. Owing to the present imperfect law under which the collectors operate, it is impractible to collect toll on the entire commerce of the river."

Between 1875 and 1898 the U. S. Army Corps of Engineers, as authorized by Congress, built a system of ten locks and dams on the Kanawha assuring year-round navigation.

During this period the Corps' Charleston office, in a yearly report to its headquarters in Washington, began to list the boats operating on the river as well as the tonnage and types of items shipped. As each of the lock and dams were completed the items shipped through them were recorded including the number of passengers carried.

Selected reports are included to illustrate the number, type and names of boats that ran on the

Kanawha. Also listed are the items shipped to provide insight into the types of commerce that prevailed in the valley.

In an 1886 report by the U.S. Army Corps of Engineers to address commerce on the river and how it would be improved with the construction of locks and dams, the following facts are related concerning packet trade for 1875, 1880 and 1886:

FREIGHT AND PASSENGER STEAMERS

"The following information, collected since your instructions of November 10 were received, in reference to the number and business of the Great Kanawha packet-boats—freight and passengers—is also submitted:

Number of packets in the trade in—

1875	6
1880	6
1886	10

The Great Kanawha packets have handled in the Kanawha trade during the twelve months ending December 1, 1886, about 41,000 tons of miscellaneous freight, mostly merchandise, farm produce, and the like. They have carried within the same time, as appears from their books, 59,355 passengers.

While coal is, of course, much the most important interest, the benefits of the completed improvement to the general freight and passenger business should not be overlooked. This trade (as appears from the statistics given) is already of considerable importance. In addition to local packets, to some of which special reference has been made, there are four good steamers running regularly, except when prevented by low water, between the Upper Great Kanawha and points on the Ohio. One of them runs to Cincinnati, and one to Pittsburgh. Both of these are handsome, well-managed packets, of about 300 tons burden, and fitted up for about 70 passengers. They carry a great deal of freight and at low rates. The rates from Cincinnati to Charleston (263 miles) on general freight, as merchandise, etc., are from 10 to 15 cents per 100; from Pittsburgh (320 miles), about 15 and 20 cents per 100. The other two steamers in the trade to the Ohio run to points near the mouth of the Great Kanawha—Gallipolis, Pomeroy, etc. They make daily trips, carrying a good deal of freight and considerable many passengers. The reliable navigation to result from a completion of the locks and dams will, undoubtedly, encourage and develop very much this general steamboat trade, and insure to the material benefit of important enterprises and a large and increasing community."

Charleston was the dividing point for the upper and lower Kanawha River trades with packets of various sizes making stops at all of the public landings and private landing when signaled.

On the upper Kanawha between Charleston and Montgomery the packets made landings at Malden (Salines), Marmet (Brownstown), Cabin Creek, Cedar Grove, Hansford (Clifton), and Pratt (Dego).* Possible family farm landings included Dickinson, Shrewsbury, Morris, Ruffner, Tompkins, Wood, Calvert, Stockton, Donnally, Venable, Noyes, Reynolds, Putney and others.

From Charleston to Winfield on the lower Kanawha the public landings were Spring Hill, St. Albans (Coalsmouth), Poca, Raymond City and Black Betsy. The family farm landing included Summers, Stewart, Thompson, Morgan, Simms, Rush, Bowling, Dudding, Wright, Mason, Webb, Swann, Lewis, Tompkins, Shelton, Blackwood, Mom's, Blain and Cobb.

Business trips could be combined with social life for the traveler on the packets. The boats became the meeting place for people living on opposite sides of the river, so that the river that was often a barrier between people, became the source of social unity. Many courtships were started on the boats and the captains and crew were always ready to introduce young and old.

Packets running in the same trade competed actively for passengers and freight. This competition often led to price rate wars. On one occasion when the steamers *Mountaineer* and *T. D. Dale* were running daily between Winfield and Charleston, the price for the trip dropped to 10¢ per trip. The packets would often race the twenty-five miles upstream to Charleston pausing only to stop at the public landings, private

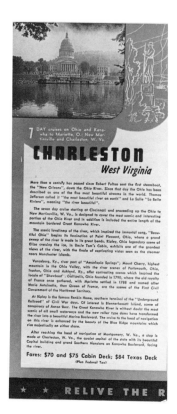

landings when hailed and to lock through old lock and dam Nos. 8, 7, and 6. The racing was very heated between the boat crews as well as the patrons with the skills of the pilots tested due to the increased speed and maneuvering. More than once races ended in accidents or near accidents.

However, as a general rule the packet boats went about their daily task in much the same manner as the modern towboats do on the rivers today, providing a service to the public. Some with a little more flair and grace than others, but all owned and crewed by men living in the communities they served.

The end of the packet boat era on the Great Kanawha River did not occur quickly but just seemed to fade away. The trade that had been established in the 1820's and 1830's were beginning to be lost to the train and the truck by the turn of the century. However the packet trade on the Kanawha was good enough that the last regular Charleston-Pittsburgh packet, the *Liberty*, did not cease operations until 1936.

Before and after the end of the packet trade the Kanawha had always been a good excursion boat river. The *Gordon C. Greene* carried overnight passengers to Charleston until 1947 and the *Avalon* was the last steamboat to operate above Winfield Locks running day and moonlight excursions until 1961.

*former town names in parentheses

REGULAR KANAWHA RIVER AND GALLIPOLIS PACKET!

The new and elegant Passenger Steamer,

COTTAGE NO. 2,

JESSE WALTON, Master. J. H. STRATTON Clerk

Leaves Gallipolis every Monday, Wednesday, and Friday at 3 A. M.
Leaves Brownstown every Tuesday, Thursday, and Saturday at 6 A. M.
The Cottage will make a trip to Pomeroy every other Saturday night.
For freight or passage apply on board.
Nov28-48-tf

Sternwheel steamers *Cottage No. 2*, *Victor No. 3*, and *Lida Norvell* were all built and operated during the Civil War. Peace found them competing in the Kanawha River trade.

REGULAR CANNELTON, KANAWHA, AND CINCINNATI PACKET.

Capt. S. C. FARLEY.
J. L. VANCE, Clerk.

Apl 8th, 1866.

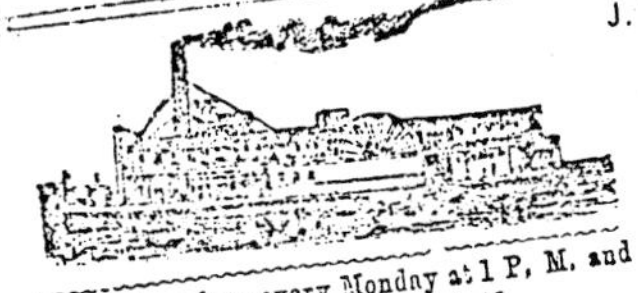

Mr D. Murray

To Steamer COTTAGE No. 2, Dr.

Leaves Cannelton every Monday at 1 P. M. and
Charleston every Tuesday at 9 A. M.
Leaves Cincinnati every Friday at 4 P. M.

MARKS.	TO FREIGHT ON	
	2 Bales Hay & tolls	$ 2 60

Paid

WM. L. MADDY, Captain. REGULAR GALLIPOLIS AND KANAWHA PACKET. H. W. GOODWIN, Clerk.

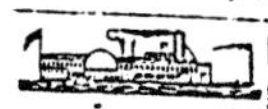

LEAVES GALLIPOLIS, Monday, Wednesday & Friday, at 5 o'clock, A. M.
LEAVES CAMP PIATT, KANAWHA RIVER, Tuesday, Thursday & Saturday, at 5 o'clock, A. M.

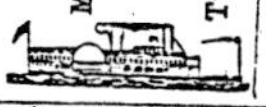

March 14 1866.

Mr A. B. Coleman

To Steamer VICTOR No. 3, Dr.

MARKS.	TO FREIGHT ON	
	10 [illegible] Corn [illegible]	4 75

Received Payment,

GALLIPOLIS & KANAWHA
REGULAR
TRI-WEEKLY PACKET
LIDA NORVELL.
TO CANNELTON EVERY FRIDAY,
L. D. WATSON, Master.

[illegible] June 1867

Mr D Murray

To Steamer LIDA NORVELL, Dr.

For Freight On

60 Bus Corn
6 Gunnies 30
13 Gunnies Retn
Less deduction

Received Payment,

E. B. [illegible]

WVSA

Charleston *June 16th* 1867

Mr Robt Carr

To Steamer **ANNIE LAURIE, Dr.**

Capt. A. O. THAYER.   W. T. THAYER, Clerk.
Leaves Cincinnati every TUESDAY at 4 P. M.
Leaves Charleston every MONDAY at 9 A. M.

G. N. MORRIS, STEAM PR., WALNUT ST.

Marks.	To Freight on		
	Passage from Pt Pleasant	$2	50

Clerk.

The beautiful and popular *Annie Laurie* spent her entire career as a Kanawha River packet.

The *Mollie Norton* only operated on the Kanawha for a short time. She spent most of her time running in the Henderson Kentucky-Evansville, Indiana trade.

Pages from the 1869 log book for steamer *Mountain Belle.*

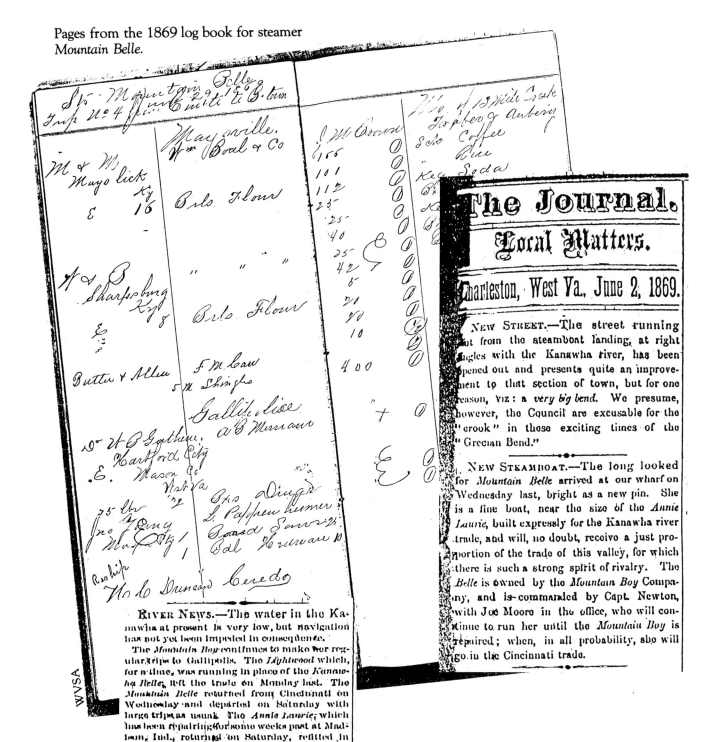

The Journal.
Local Matters.

Charleston, West Va., June 2, 1869.

NEW STREET.—The street running out from the steamboat landing, at right angles with the Kanawha river, has been opened out and presents quite an improvement to that section of town, but for one reason, viz: a *very big bend*. We presume, however, the Council are excusable for the "crook" in these exciting times of the "Grecian Bend."

NEW STEAMBOAT.—The long looked for *Mountain Belle* arrived at our wharf on Wednesday last, bright as a new pin. She is a fine boat, near the size of the *Annie Laurie*, built expressly for the Kanawha river trade, and will, no doubt, receive a just proportion of the trade of this valley, for which there is such a strong spirit of rivalry. The *Belle* is owned by the *Mountain Boy* Company, and is commanded by Capt. Newton, with Joe Moore in the office, who will continue to run her until the *Mountain Boy* is repaired; when, in all probability, she will go in the Cincinnati trade.

RIVER NEWS.—The water in the Kanawha at present is very low, but navigation has not yet been impeded in consequence.

The *Mountain Boy* continues to make her regular trips to Gallipolis. The *Lightwood* which, for a time, was running in place of the *Kanawha Belle*, left the trade on Monday last. The *Mountain Belle* returned from Cincinnati on Wednesday and departed on Saturday with large trips as usual. The *Annie Laurie*, which has been repairing for some weeks past at Madison, Ind., returned on Saturday, refitted in good style, presenting an appearance as good as new. She left on Monday for Cincinnati, loaded with salt. The *Kanawha Belle* made her appearance again on Sunday, having been on the docks at Cincinnati repairing. She still sticks to her motto, "root hog or die," and re-entered the Gallipolis trade on Monday. Several low boats passed up and down the river during the week.

THE *Active*, that fine light draught boat, is still plying regularly in the up river trade. We trust that she is now one of the fixed institutions. Mondays, Wednesdays and Fridays are her up river days. For freight or passage apply on board.

Local news stories indicate the importance of a new street to the steamboat landing and the arrival of the new steamboat, the *Mountain Belle*, to the city.

River news was carried as a regular feature in all local newspapers.

MR. E. MARTIN, of Kanawha Salines, has been appointed Mail Route messenger on the Kanawha river in charge of the U. S. mail on the *Mountain Boy.* Capt. John H. Rosler, the late agent, will enter at once upon the duties as assistant assessor of Internal Revenue for this County.

STEAM BOAT ACCIDENT.—Our young friend, Alex. Summers, one of the engineers, of the hitherto fortunate Steamboat "Annie Laurie," furnished us with the following particulars in reference to the sinking of the *Annie Laurie,* a fine passenger steamer on Wednesday morning last, about 7 o'clock, plying between Charleston and Cincinnati while entering the chute in "Nob" Shoals of the Kanawha river, immediately above Buffalo, struck the left hand wall and broke a hole in her hull about ten feet long, which caused her to sink in less than an hour. The "Mountain Belle" from Gallipolis arrived in time to receive all deck freight except the salt, which was all lost. All the passengers were safely transferred to the "Mountain Belle" and were taken on to Gallipolis without very much delay by the accident. There was about 1100 barrels of salt lost, and also a slight damage on about 30 hogsheads of tobacco. Everything else was saved without injury. Preparations are being made to raise the wreck at once; it will take some time however, to do it. The back water from the Ohio and the thick fog so completely blinded the walls that it evidently was not the fault of Ed. Johnson, the pilot, who is an old hand in the business. The loss of the "Laurie" is greatly felt.

A good opening now for some fine boat for the Cincinnati trade.

1869 *West Virginia Journal* advertisements and articles covering *Annie Laurie* accident and her replacement boat, *W. F. Curtis.*

Steamer *W. F. Curtis* was built in 1864 at Parkersburg and ran in the Pittsburgh-Gallipolis trade. Burned in 1867, was rebuilt and ran lower Ohio River trades, then Mississippi River trades. Her brief Kanawha River service, filling in for the *Annie Laurie*, was just prior to going south to the Mississippi River.

THE river is in fine boating stage and is rising gradually. The probability is if there should be high water now, the *Annie Laurie* will be seriously injured, and that the work of raising her will be retarded in consequence.

MR. HILL, the wharf master, informs us that the steamer *W. F. Curtis* will be here during the week to fill the place of the *Annie Laurie* in the Cincinnati trade.

While 1870 and 1871 issues of the *Point Pleasant Register* were carrying packet boat advertisements, an 1870 issue of the *West Virginia Journal*
was announcing the largest flatboat ever to run
on the Kanawha had sailed to Paducah,
Kentucky.

Flatboats continued to run until well after the
turn of the century.

Newspapers of the 1870's often had half pages filled with packet advertisements competing for the Kanawha River and connecting Ohio River customers.

Note the names of the boats that connections were made with.

Named for the superintendent of the Murraysville, West Virginia boat yard where she was built in 1871, the *R. W, Skillinger* first ran in the Pittsburgh-Portsmouth trade on the Ohio River. She was sold to Captain S. C. Farley and others and operated briefly on the Kanawha. Sold again in 1872 to run as a Wheeling-Cincinnati packet, she burned at Cincinnati in 1875, probably hit by lightning during a storm.

Photograph by Dr. Claudius M. Pitrat at Buffalo, West Virginia, 1871.

Note banner on boiler deck railing announcing her as a Kanawha River Packet.

Entered according to Act of Congress, in the year 1869, by IRA DRESSER, in the Clerk's Office of the District Court of the U. S., for the Southern District of Ohio.

Regular Wheeling and Cincinnati Packet.

Steamer R. W. Skillinger.

Capt. J. T. Russell,   C. R. Russell, Clerk.

CABIN PASSAGE TICKET

To..

Keep this Ticket in sight at Table.

GOOD FOR THIS TRIP ONLY.

Leaves Wheeling every Monday at 3 P. M.
Leaves Cincinnati every Thursday at 5 P. M.

.............................Clerk.

Entered according to Act of Congress in the year 1872, by IRA DRESSER, in the Office of the Librarian of Congress, at Washington.

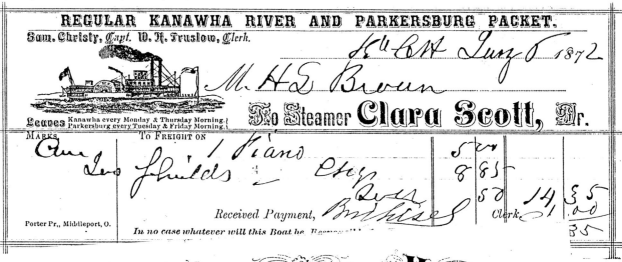

REGULAR KANAWHA RIVER AND PARKERSBURG PACKET.

Sam. Christy, Capt. W. H. Truslow, Clerk.

[handwritten] 16th CH July 5 1872

M. H. S. Brown

To Steamer **Clara Scott, Dr.**

Leaves Kanawha every Monday & Thursday Morning. Parkersburg every Tuesday & Friday Morning.

MARKS	TO FREIGHT ON		
[handwritten] Clay Geo Shields	1 Piano	5 00	
	2 Boxes	8 85	
	[handwritten]	50	14 35

Received Payment, *[signature]* Clerk.

Porter Pr., Middleport, O.

In no case whatever will this Boat be ————

HALE HOUSE
CHARLESTON, W.A.

H. W. REYNOLDS, SUPT.

W. B. CLARKSON, CLERK.

187___

——:o:——

ACCIDENT TO THE SCOTT—
TELEGRAPH DOWN.—As the Clara
Scott was passing up the river yesterday morning, her chimneys
caught the telegraph wires stretch-
ed across the river to the hill opposite town, and besides tearing
down the wires, tore down her
chimneys; one of which falling
upon the pilot house caused considerable damage. She proceeded
at once to Thayer's foundry where
her injuries were repaired. The
telegraph pole on this side of the
river which stands in front of the
store of Messrs. W. F. and J. W.
Goshorn, was pulled over against
the building knocking several
bricks from the coping. We understand that the injury to the
wires will be repaired to-day,
workmen having been ordered
here for that purpose. Meanwhile,
the operator at the Hale House
will continue to receive and deliver messages by means of the
battery at the Depot

The *Clara Scott* ran in the Parkersburg-Charleston
trade from 1871 to 1875.

In May 1875 Chief of the U.S. Army Corps of
Engineers, Andrew A. Humphreys, along with a board
of engineers inspected the Kanawha River on the *Scott*.
The inspection ended with a banquet at the Hale
House in Charleston and led to Congress approving
funds for the construction of locks and dams.

On her return trip downstream, the *Scott* sank in
seven feet of water, but none of her distinguished
guests were aboard.

Her wreck lay at Island Chute, below Charleston
and as late as 1921 part was said to be visible.

Steamer *Clara Scott* at a Kanawha River landing, probably Buffalo.

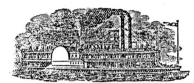
The *Here's Your Mule* was built at Buffalo, New York in 1866 on a hull 51.1x9.8x2.8. She was a propeller driven steamer that operated in connection with the *Mocking Bird*.

The *Phil Morgan* was built at Charleston, West Virginia in 1871 and worked as either a towboat or packet. Note 1872 *Charleston City Directory* advertisement.

The *Mocking Bird* was a small propeller driven steam packet that was built at Buffalo, New York. She only operated on the upper Kanawha for a few years before being sold.

The *Kittie Hegler* was built in 1871 to replace the *Annie Laurie*. She was replaced by the *Julia No. 2* after only a couple of years on the Kanawha.

Built in 1860 at Parkersburg, the small *Bettie Gilbert* ran trades on both the upper and lower Kanawha until 1873.

She was dismantled at Metropolis, Illinois in 1889 with her machinery going to a hub factory.

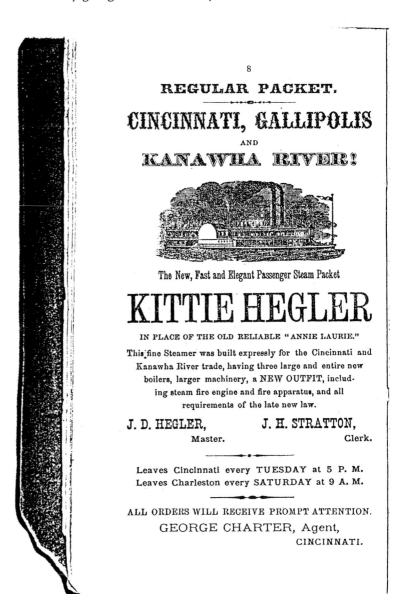

Page from the 1872 *Charleston City Directory.*

Soon to be the nemesis of the packet trade, this ad for the C & O Railroad dated 1872 is apparently the first announcing railroad travel to and from Charleston.

In the years before "standard" time was put into effect there were once as many as 56 time "zones" in a patchwork quilt across the country.

Facing Page — The steamer *Active* photographed by Dr. Claudius M. Pitrat at Buffalo on the Kanawha. She ran between Charleston and Cannelton, located opposite Coal Valley (Montgomery) on the upper Kanawha. Later ran as a Charleston-Gallipolis packet.

} Kanawha and Gallipolis Tri-weekly Packet. { Leaves Gallipolis,
Tuesdays, Thursdays and Saturdays.

WM. HIX, Captain.

Pt Pleast July 10th 1873.

M. A. Bickle

To Steamer ACTIVE, Dr

To Freight on 1 Bex Ale Chs Consumers 6 50 6 75

Butter

Received Payment, Clerk.

UNITED STATES INTERNAL REVENUE.
RETURN FOR SPECIAL TAX.

[Every person or firm liable to Special Tax must, on or before the 30th day of April of each year, or before comm
business, if such business is commenced subsequent to April 30th, file with the Collector or Deputy Collector a sworn return
form, and pay to such officer the amount of the tax, when he will be furnished with a *Special-Tax Stamp*, which must be at a
conspicuously displayed in his or their place of business.]

STATE OF West. Va.

COUNTY OF Kanawha,

The undersigned _William Wise, Captain_
of Str. Active _that on the_
being duly sworn according to law, declare that on the
_____ 187 he w engaged in, [or] intend on the
day of May _____, 1873, to engage in, the business or o
Retail Liquor & Manuft. Toba
Dealer
said firm consisting of the following named persons _Steamer_
_____
subject to special tax under the Internal Revenue Laws of the United State
or occupation to be carried on at No. _Kanawha & Ohio River_
the _____ and State of _____

of _____
that he
liable to

SWORN
day

To

Bill of Sale,
OF THE 6/15
STEAM BOAT,

Active

I.H. Stratton & W.Hix

—TO—

J.O. Reynolds

Received and recorded at the Custom House,

Parkersburg, W. Va, Sept 2st 1872

at 8 o'clock A.M.,

in Vol. One Page 201 & 202

TRIP STATEMENT.

Steamer Active   Trip No. One

From March 29th to _____ and Return.

April 6th 1873

Freight,	278	10	Wages,	229	00
Passengers,	194	10	Expenses,	47	47
Bar Rent	7	79	Stores,	109	76
Mail Service	25	00	Fuel,	53	05
Total,	504	99	Total,	439	28

RECAPITULATION.

Total Amount Receipts,	504	99
Total Amount Expenses,	439	28
Profit,	$65	71

REMARKS:

Capt N.B. Coleman
The above is the Exebit
of Last week's business.
Respectfully
A.J. Beckett

— 62 —

November 1, 1873 *Charleston Daily Courier* account of the steamer *Julia No. 2's* arrival at Charleston after an extended low water period. So important was the *Julia No. 2's* trip that the entire manifest was printed. Built at Wellsville, Ohio in 1865, the *Julia No. 2* came to the Kanawha River in 1872 by Captain J. V. Reynolds until he built the *Virgie Lee* in 1876.

The impact of prolonged periods of low water or ice on the river are clearly illustrated by this news story on the economy of the valley. Occurrences such as this helped bring about the building of the locks and dams on the Kanawha.

Charleston Daily Courier, November 1, 1873.

——— :o: ———

MAMIFEST OF THE JULIA NO. 2.—Steamer Julia No. 2, in port Saturday morning:

R R Skees, 357 packages furniture; Kanawha Flour Mills, 234 sacks corn; J W M Appleton, 10 hearth stones; King, Ewing & Hoback, 18 do; E M Stone, 14 do; E F Dunne, 8 do; C H Small 190 cases and packages earthenware, etc.; W F Herbert & Co., 5 cases; J R Hodgson, 27 barrels and cases groceries; Ruffner Bros., 7 barrels and cases goods; Nick Mason, 2 cases; Ruby & Hale, 270 cases and merchandise; G. Sloth, 1 barrel bacon; B Ward, 1 do, and package casting; H Reed, 2 trucks lard and bacon and barrel beef; C. B. Co., 40 sks. malt; Houser & Whipple, ½ barrel plaster; H Wehrle, lot grapes; L L Comstock, 1 phæton; S S Moore, lot frames, etc.; H S Walker, 10 bundles paper, k g ink; Jelenko Bros., 77 cases and packages merchandise; E Laughorn, 408 chairs; G T Barlow, 4 tables; W W Riley, 7 boxes and casks goods; J T Reynolds, 3 do; J C Riley, 3 do; J T Copenhaver, 3 do; Mrs. S C Farley, lot beds and hardware; M J Bell & Co., 5 barrels plaster; J M Gates & Bro., 25 barrels lime; Capt. Woodward, lot blinds and hardware; O A & W T Thayer, 5 tons pig iron; A H Wilson. 20 cases, etc., hardware; G Ritter & Co., 6 do; John A Truslow, 6 packages leather, etc.; W. F. & J H Goshorn, 44 cases, etc., hardware; Jos. Bohnert, 5 do.

——— •••• ———

——— :o: ———

A REVIVAL.—The Julia No 2 which arrived here on Thursday night brought up a magnificent manifest from down the river and especially from Cincinnati. Although there has been a great falling off freight from Cincinnati since the panic and low water, there had accumulated a great deal of freight in that city ready for shipment to this place and to other points along the Kanawha; which, as long as low water lasted, the shippers feared to send, unless by some reliable Kanawha Packet.

The same was the case along the river in regard to shipments *to* Cincinnati, and hence it was that the Julia went into Cincinnati loaded down to the very water's edge and that she left there equally as well loaded. By reference to her manifest printed elsewhere, it will be seen that our river trade is looking up, for besides her manifest for this city she distributed freight, all the way up. Her passenger lists both ways were excellent. Our people generally and especially our merchants must hail the good stage of water with delight, and many who grumbled and complained that their Fall stock was incomplete, have now an opportunity to fill their stores with any quantity of merchandise.

MARKS.	ARTICLES.	WEIGHTS.
A B Co	8 Bbls Sugar	2202
	2 " Vinegar	700
	10 Bags Coffee	1342
	2 Kegs Soda	250
	1 Bag Pepper	124
	½ " Allspice	57
	½ Cask Tea	80
	3 Box Candles	120
	" Candy	100
	2 Doz 2H Pails	120
	4 Netts (4) Mkt Baskets	10
	2 Doz Wash Boards	120
	4 Kegs Nquees	801
	23 " Lard	1174
	3 Bbls Molasses	1500
	2 " Miners Oil	700
	1 " Engine "	350
	3 " Carbon "	1050
	7 Hhd CR Bulk Sides	1550
	2 " Bulk Shlds	

RENEWAL OF LIFE.—Since the rains there has been a decided renewal of life on the river. There is about five feet eight inches in the channel, just about twice as much water as before the rains, and up to Saturday evening late (we don't write locals on Sunday) it was still rising gradually. The water is excellent for boating now, and from all accounts the Ohio is even better now, though it will hardly last as long as in the Kanawha. On Saturday morning it seemed like old times to see the Clara Scott, Julia No. 2 and Daniel Boone all leaving for down the river about the same time. They went respectively to Parkersburg, Cincinnati and Gallipolis.

Soon after they left the Alex. Chambers came down with several salt and coal barges heavily laden. The Modoc moved out and went up the river for some barges, and in the afternoon the Lookout came up, bringing some empty ones, which she left at the mouth of Elk. The Ianthe and Shoo Fly, which have had things their own way since the big boats had to lay up, were running around snorting and blowing like two little terriers when a big dog fight is going on. Everything is encouraging and the "anserial elevation is lofty."

Renewal of life was a very appropriate lead to the news article on the beginning of commerce after an extended low water period on the Kanawha. When the boats stopped running, business stopped with them.

The steam towboat *Alex Chambers* was built in 1864 at West Brownsville, Pennsylvania and had the distinction of bringing the first locomotive for the Hocking Valley Railroad from Parkersburg to Gallipolis.

The *Modoc* and the *Lookout* worked as combination packet boats/towboats based on the information found during research for this book.

Although the *Modoc* operated as a packet in 1875 and 1878 (see facing page), she was registered as a towboat in Wheeling in 1881-1882.

The *Ianthe* and *Shoo Fly* were ferryboats that operated in the Charleston area.

M. J. BELL & CO.,

Forwarding and Commission Merchants and Wharf-Boat Proprietors,

CHARLESTON, WEST VA.

Shipped, in good order and well conditioned, by

M. J. BELL & CO.,

On board the good Steamboat _Modoc_ now lying at the Port of CHARLESTON, the following articles, marked and numbered as below, which are to be delivered, without delay, in like GOOD ORDER and condition, at the Port of _____ (the unavoidable dangers of Navigation and Fire only excepted.) unto _____, or assigns, he or they paying freight and charges for said goods as specified. Rate, $_____

IN WITNESS WHEREOF, The Owner, Agent, Master or Clerk of said Boat hath affirmed to Three Bills of Lading of this tenor and date, one of which being accomplished, the others to stand void.

Dated at Charleston, this _2 2_ day of _July_, 187_8_

MARKS.	ARTICLES.	WEIGHTS.
M T C Sundries	22 Empty Bags Chge $8.00 (Freight $1.10)	

Charleston Feb 18, 1878

Mr David Murray

To Steamer **MODOC,** Dr.

In no case whatever will the Boat be responsible for Freight after she leaves the Landing.

Marks.	To Freight on		
	3 Bales Hay	75	

Received Payment,

Regular Gallipolis and Kanawha River Tri-Weekly Packet.

GOES THROUGH TO POMEROY EVERY SATURDAY.   J. A. McClurg, Clerk.

R. L. Hamilton, Master.

Leaves Gallipolis for Kanawha every Monday, Wednesday & Friday at 3 a. m.
Leaves Charleston for Gallipolis every Tuesday, Thursday & Saturday at 8 a. m.

_N 3_   187_5_

Mr Wm Keely

To Steamer **DANIEL BOONE,** Dr.

In no case whatever will the Boat be responsible for Freight after she leaves the Landing.

Marks.	To Freight on				
	2 Bale Hay	585#	6	43	
	9 Bag Meal L24¢		90	10	7	43

Clerk.

Received Payment,

Built in 1871 as a Pittsburgh-Morgantown packet on the Monongahela River, the *West Virginia* entered the Gallipolis-Charleston trade in 1876. Captain J. B. Dudding sold her to the upper Ohio River in 1878 and bought the *Telephone* to take her place.

W. O. Martin, Captain.
A. J. Becket, Clerk.

Leaves Kanawha for Gallipolis
Every Monday, Wednesday & Friday morning
Leaves Gallipolis for Kanawha
Every Monday, Wednesday and Friday night.

Regular Kanawha River and Gallipolis Packet.

Freight and Passengers Receipted through to all Points between Gallipolis and Pittsburgh or Cincinnati at Lowest Rates.

Charleston, W. Va., June 5 , 1877

M J E Logel

Jo Steamer **WEST VIRGINIA, Dr.**

In no case whatever will this Boat be responsible for Freight after she leaves the Landing.

| MARKS. | To Freight on | 10 Bbls Flour | 1 | 50 | | |
| | | | | 30 | $ | 1.80 |

J. B. DUDDING, Captain.
A. J. BECKETT, Clerk.

LEAVES KANAWHA FOR GALLIPOLIS:
Every Monday, Wednesday and Friday Morning.
LEAVES GALLIPOLIS FOR KANAWHA:
Every Monday, Wednesday and Friday Night.

JAS. P. GEPPERT, PR., CIN'TI.

REGULAR KANAWHA RIVER AND GALLIPOLIS PACKET.

Freight and Passengers Receipted through to all points between Gallipolis and Pittsburgh, or Cincinnati, at Lowest Rates.

Snow Hill March 21st 1878.

M Snow Hill Salt Co,

To Steamer WEST VIRGINIA, Dr.

In no case whatever will this boat be responsible for Freight after she leaves the Landing.

MARKS.	To Freight		FREIGHT.	CHARGES.	AMOUNT.	
	566# Butter				70	75
87 Bbls Salt						
88 4/10					8	8.40

Received Payment,

Clerk.

— 66 —

1878 handbill for the new steamer *Telephone.* Note the message at the bottom of the handbill.

Built at Portsmouth, Ohio, the *Telephone* began operations five weeks after the world's first commercial telephone exchange opened at New Haven, Connecticut, so the owners named their new boat after a subject fresh on the public's mind.

First year ran Pittsburgh-Cincinnati, then Wheeling-Charleston trade. Later as a Gallipolis-Charleston packet and later resumed the Wheeling-Charleston run. Sank on January 2, 1886 from ice damage.

THE EXCURSION PARTY.—On Sunday about 11 a. m., the splendid side-wheel steamer "City of Portsmouth," hove in sight and was soon at the wharf, just below the levee. We have already described this steamer and given the details of her dimensions, power, &c. Some few weeks ago she made her first trip up to this place and at that time brought up about one hundred and fifty passengers, who had laid aside business and other toil to spend Sunday "excurting" up and down our beautiful valley. Captain Bryan and Frank Morgan, the clerk, are among the most popular steamboatmen on the Ohio, and we are assured by some of the excursionists that everything to make these trips successes was done. After landing a good many persons at the wharf, the steamer went on up the river some distance to enable the party to view the beautiful and picturesque scenery, which greets the eye in varied attractiveness at every turn of the Kanawha. Although everything now is rather in the sere and melancholy bareness of winter, there is still enough beauty to reward the curious from a distance. Those who stopped over here spent the day in walking around and becoming acquainted with the principal points of interest. The majority of them registered at the Hale House, where they found a hotel and host unequaled in this State. A bountiful dinner, as usual, greeted the party and judging from the lingering regrets they manifested at leaving Col. Wood, we presume they found it a far more charming place than their wildest expectations had led them to believe. At about 7 p. m., the steamer returned from up the river and after giving the signal of departure, soon steamed away out of sight with her happy passengers. As these trips have proven so popular, we daresay we may expect many more during the spring and summer. There were about two hundred passengers aboard on this trip.

The rich heritage of the Kanawha River excursion boats can trace their beginnings to the *City of Portsmouth* excursions as related in the June 8, 1874 issue of the *Charleston Daily Courier*.

THE BOATS.—The Julia took took down her usual large manifest on Saturday, although the rivers are quite low.

The Scott and Active leave this morning. We hear that of late the boats have had rather a dull season with freights though the passenger lists have been good.

The Boone comes up this afternoon.

A good many tow boats are lying up on account of low water.

Not all news was good news on the river. The *Julia* accident occured at the "Elk Chute," the same place the steamer *Senator Cordill* would ground for about three weeks in 1927.

AN ACCIDENT TO THE JULIA.—On Saturday about noon, the Julia left here heavily laden, for Cincinnatr In passing down through the chute at the mouth of Elk, she grounded the head of the boat, and swinging around, sprung the starboard dead wood and had to ground. She took in some little water and sustained but little damage. The injury to the cargo, which belonged principally to the boat, was slight. The rumors on the street Saturday evening were exaggerated, though they grew as they passed from mouth to mouth, we are informed by those present at the time of the accident, that the injury to boat and cargo was very slight. We regret the accident to this popular boat, and are satisfied that no officers could be more prompt or efficient than those of the Julia About 4 p. m., she got off and continued on down the river, and no doubt will come up this week as strong and safe as ever.

The blowing of steamboat whistles within the city limits is the subject of both a city ordinance forbidding the whistling and an editorial concernng the ordinance.

THE STEAMBOAT WHISTLING.

We noticed among the proceedings of the City Council, at their last meeting, that a petition had been presented to that body by the Kanawha B.ard, in relation to rescinding the ordinance forbidding the whistling of steamboats within the corporation. This ordinance was passed several years ago and went by default, nobody seeming to take steps to prevent the eternal nuisance of steamboats whistling and blowing, sometimes for five or ten minutes. Had they only whistled in moderation, just as they were landing or about to leave—or, in other words, had they not abused the privilege—we would never have been requested to ask a revival and enforcement of the ordinance, which request proved successful. But they did abuse, it and annoyed everybody within hearing. Sick people living along the river's bank were almost crazed by this nuisance, while business men were deafened by the abuse of the privilege. There has been one violation of the ordinance since its revival, no doubt, through forgetfulness on the part of those offending. A fine was imposed, and since that time abuse has been heaped upon the Council, verbally and in some of the newspapers, by those who wished steamboats to continue their abomniable whistling. If steamboatmen seek to bid for public patronage by such action, alike hostile to their own interests and those of the public, the sooner they were told in plain words of their mistake the better. To be brief, if steamboatmen, whether owners or officers, attempt to override public comfort and when prevented array themselves against the people,

the issue will be of their own making, and they must not be surprised if their former patronage is transferred to those boats which submit to a consideration of those people whose patronage is the life of their trade.

It would be well for them to think of this. No city or town of our size submits to such nuisances, as we have for years, and ninety-nine hundreths of the citizens endorse the action of the Council. Show us a man who advocates this unlimited whistling, and we will show one to whom personal and pecuniary considerations are greater than the comfort of the whole community, whether sick or not. No doubt a strong pressure will be brought against the Council to rescind their ordinance by these petitions, but we have faith that they knew what they were doing when they revived the ordinance, and will not permit themselves to make ordinances one day for the benefit of all, then change them the next to accommodate the purses of a few. We have no desire to say one word prejudicial to the steamboats, but between their whistling and the good of the citizens, unqualifiedly incline to the latter, and this is the basis of this article. We have no idea that the Council will rescind the ordinance, but our chief object is to assure them that they will have the unqualified support of the citizens in enforcing it, and if they should in an indiscreet moment rescind it, they will do themselves no less injustice than the people. We hope that while they may treat all petitions with due consideration, this one will be laid over indefinitely, or being voted upon, be emphatically denied.

The *Wild Goose* was built in 1878 to run between St. Albans and Brownstown (Marmet). She was the first of three stern-wheel boats (1 steam, 2 diesel) that were named *Wild Goose* and operated on the Kanawha. The second *Wild Goose* was built at Charleston by Ward Engineering Works in 1926 and the third was the U. S. Engineers towboat *Gillette* that was renamed *Wild Goose* when bought by Captain Harry White of Witchers Creek in 1947.

This was just one of the boats that operated on the Kanawha that had an colorful name. Some of the others were *Lame Duck, John Go 'Long, Here's Your Mule, Tuckahoe* and *Tiskilwa*.

Usually running in the Gallipolis-Kanawha River trade, the *Boone* sometimes ran Ohio River trips. She sank and was lost while enroute from Cincinnati to Charleston when Captain Zenus Baxter ran the *Boone* close to the bank to throw a newspaper ashore at his home near Sciotoville, Ohio and hit a snag. Her passengers and freight were taken off by the steamer *Louise* who then continued to run on her Kanawha River trade.

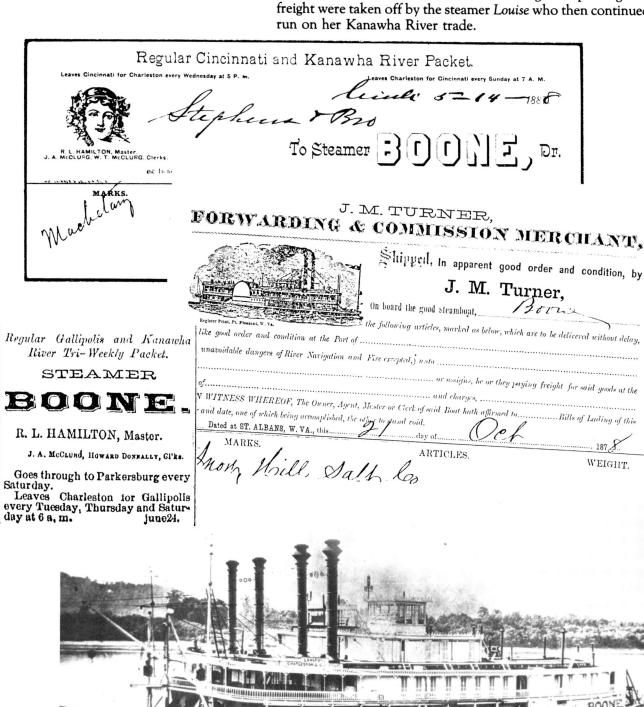

Built to replace the *Julia No. 2* in the Kanawha River-Cincinnati trade in 1876, the *Virgie Lee* only ran this route for two years before moving to the lower Ohio River. Later in her career, she again ran in the Kanawha River trades and her roof bell wound up in a church at Henderson, W. Va. when she was dismantled.

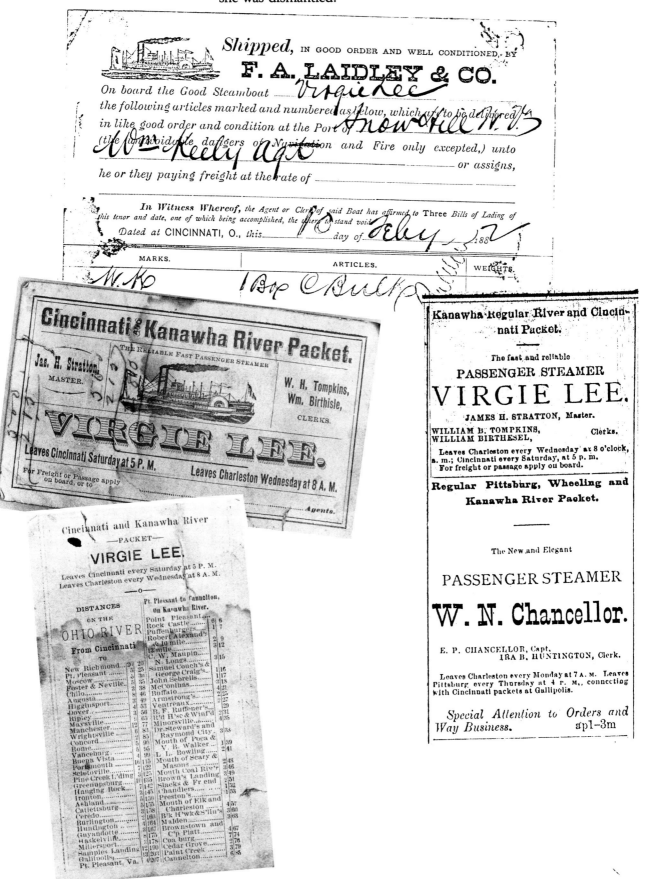

REGULAR KANAWHA RIVER, WHEELING AND PITTSBURGH PACKET

E. P. CHANCELLOR, Captain.   Leaves CHARLESTON every _____ at 7 A. M.   IRA B. HUNTINGTON, Clerk.
                               Leaves PITTSBURGH every _____ at 4 P. M.

Thompson & Jackson   *Parkersburgh Nov 21   185*

To Steamer **W. N. CHANCELLOR,** Dr.

MARKS.	To Freight on	Freight.	Charges.	Amount.

Regular Kanawha River, Wheeling and Pittsburgh Passenger Packet.

Leaves CHARLESTON Mondays at 6 A. M.
Leaves PITTSBURGH Thursdays at 4 P. M.

W. A. Long   *Songs Aug 1   188 1*

E. P. CHANCELLOR, Master.
IRA B. HUNTINGTON, Clerk.

W. W. PIKE, PR. CIN.

To Steamer **W. N. Chancellor,** Dr.

MARKS.	To Freight on	Freight.	Charges.	Amount.
	400 Ps Sewer Pipe			*$37.50*

Received Payment.   *Ira B Huntington*   Clerk.

The *W. N. Chancellor* was the first regular Pittsburgh and Kanawha River packet, pioneering the trade in 1881. Named for a prominent West Virginian who was the Democratic candidate for the state's governor in 1896, this packet was built in 1879 and ran on the Kanawha until 1892. The Pittsburgh-Charleston trade proved to be so lucrative that packet boats would run it until the end of the packet era, when the *Liberty* made her last trip between the two cities in 1936.

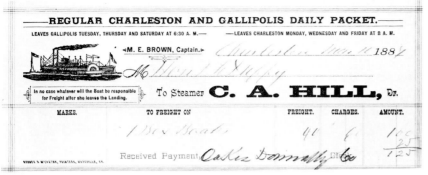

The C. A. *Hill* began as a Gallipolis-Charleston packet when built in 1884. Later ran in the Gallipolis-Pomeroy-Syracuse trade on the Ohio River before being sold south.

Steamer *Louise* when she was new in 1882 ran twice weekly between Marietta-Parkersburg-Charleston, going up the Kanawha to Coal Valley (Montgomery).

She took the freight from the sunken *Boone* in 1888 and then took the *Boone's* place in the Cincinnati-Charleston trade.

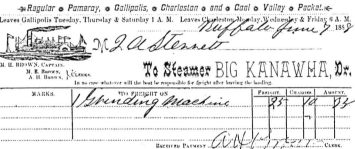

The *Big Kanawha* was a packet built for the Pomeroy-Gallipolis-Charleston-Coal Valley trade in 1887 but only ran there for a few years. She was then sold and ran on various Ohio River trades before being lost in heavy ice in 1906.

Steamer *Keystone State* built in 1890 for the Pittsburgh-Cincinnati packet line. Sold in 1909, the new owner took the boat to the Kanawha Dock Company at Pt. Pleasant to receive a new hull. Owner could not pay for the new hull and the *Keystone State* was attached for the debt. She remained at the dock for several years in litigation.

While running on the Ohio, there was a popular poem about the *Keystone State*:

> The *Keystone State* although a tub,
> Feeds up on the best of grub.
> I don't see how they make her pay,
> For she's so long she gets the freight
> Because she always runnin' late.

Everybody was going to the circus at Charleston on Monday, May 13, 1889 when this photograph was made at the foot of Bradford Street. The *Sonoma* left Montgomery with a large crowd aboard and in the next 26 miles she made 82 landings picking up more people at each stop. Even a brass band is on this small (115' x 20' x 3' hull) packet that has a tarpaulin draped over the bow to prevent leakage around the stem.

The *Sonoma* was built in 1881. Spent most of her career operating on the Muskingum River in Ohio. Sank in 1913.

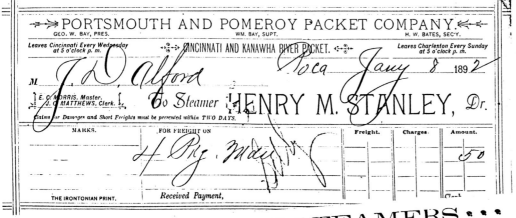

Built for the Cincinnati-Charleston trade in 1890 and named for the explorer who found Dr. David Livingstone in deepest Africa ("Dr. Livingstone, I presume"). Sold to the Greene Line steamers in 1904 who ran her in the Cincinnati-Pomeroy-Charleston trade. Sank on September 3, 1907 near Gallipolis Island.

Steamer *Henry M. Stanley*'s cabin set for dinner with turned chairs, stacked napkins and silverware under crystal decorated brass chandeliers. Luxury like this exceeded almost any hotel found on the *Stanleys*'s route.

From CINCINNATI to	Time Table—Up.	Time Table—Down.
New Richmond.......20	Passes N. Richmond.......7 30 p m	Lvs Coal Valley Saird'y..9 30 a m
Augusta.......42	" Augusta.........8 30 "	Passes Hampton........11 00 "
Ripley.......52	" Ripley, Thursday 12 30 a m	" Coalburg.......11 15 "
Maysville.......61	" Maysville.........1 30 "	" Winifrede.......11 30 "
Manchester.......72	" Manchester.........4 00 "	" Brownstown....12 00 n'n
Rome.......85	" Rome.........7 00 "	" Malden.........1 00 p m
Vanceburg.......91	" Vanceburg.........8 00 "	Lvs Charleston, Sunday..5 00 a m
Portsmouth.......113	" Portsmouth.........11 00 "	Passes St. Albans.........6 30 "
Greenup and Riverton....133	" Greenup & Rivit'n 2 00 p m	" Raymond City......7 30 "
Ironton.......141	" Ironton.........5 00 "	" Winfield & Red H.8 45 "
Ashland.......146	" Ashland.........5 00 "	" Frazier's.........9 30 "
Catlettsburg.......152	" Catlettsburg.........6 00 "	" Buffalo.........10 00 "
Kenova and Ceredo.......155	" Kenova.........6 30 "	" Maupin's.......10 40 "
Huntington.......160	" Huntington.........7 00 "	" Leon.........11 30 "
Guyandotte & Proctorsvle.163	" Guyan & Proctor..8 00 "	" Brighton.........12 00 n'n
Crown City.......178	" Crown City........10 00 "	" Pt. Pleasant......1 00 p m
Chambersburg.......189	" Chambersburg, 12 00 night	" Gallipolis.........2 00 "
Gallipolis.......200	" Gallipolis, Friday....4 a m	" Chambersburg....4 00 "
Point Pleasant.......204	" Pt. Pleasant,Ka Riv 5 00 "	" Crown City........5 00 "
Brighton—Kanaw'a River.211	" Brighton.........6 15 "	" Guyan & Proctor'r 6 00 "
Leon.......215	" Leon.........7 00 "	" Huntington.........7 00 "
Maupin's.......218	" Maupin's.........7 15 "	" Kenova & Ceredo.8 00 "
Buffalo.......225	" Buffalo.........8 15 "	" Catlettsburg.........8 30 "
Frazier's Bottom.......229	" Frazier's.........9 00 "	" Ashland.........8 30 "
Winfield and Red House..236	" Winfield & Red H 10 00 "	" Ironton.........10 30 "
Raymond City and Poca...242	" Raymond City..12 00 n'n	" Greenup, Monday.1 00 a m
St. Alban's.......249	" St. Alban's.......2 00 p m	" Portsmouth.........7 00 "
Charleston.......262	" Charleston.........4 00 "	" Vanceburg.........10 00 "
Malden.......267	" Malden.........10 00 "	" Rome.........11 00 "
Brownstown.......271	" Brownstown......11 00 "	" Manchester.....2 30 p m
Winifrede.......275	" Winifrede.......15 00 n't	" Maysville.........4 00 "
Coalburg.......278	" Hampton, Satr'dy.5 00 a m	" Ripley.........5 00 "
Hampton & Cedar Grove..281	Arrive Coal Valley & Can..7 30	" Augusta.........6 30 "
Coal Valley.......269		" New Richmond....8 30 "

Steamer *Lizzie Bay* as she appeared when new and first started in the Pittsburgh-Charleston trade. This trade was so good that the "Lousy Liz," as she was known, was lengthened and a texas added. Sold in 1895 to run in Ohio River trades. Dismantled in 1912.

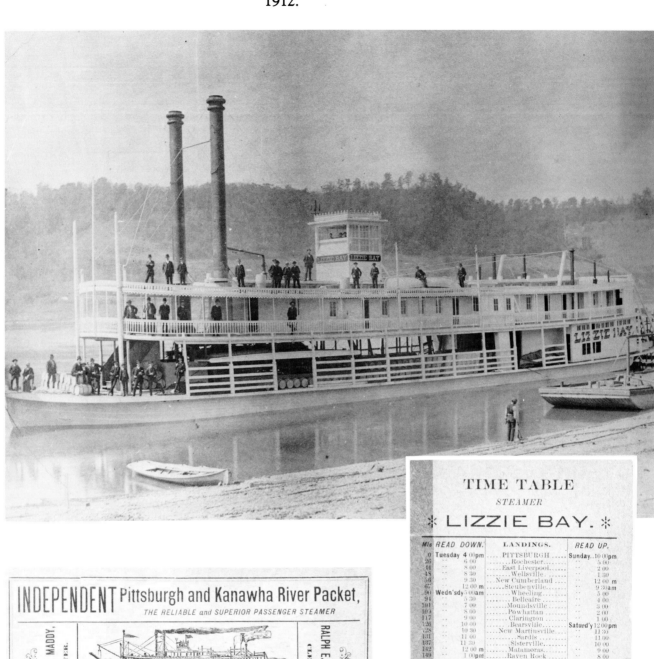

TIME TABLE
STEAMER
※ LIZZIE BAY. ※

Mls	READ DOWN.	LANDINGS.	READ UP.
0	Tuesday 4 00pm	PITTSBURGH	Sunday..10 00pm
26	6 00	Rochester	5 00
44	8 00	East Liverpool	2 00
48	8 30	Wellsville	1 30
55	9 30	New Cumberland	12 00 m
67	12 00 m	Steubenville	9 30am
90	Wedn'sdy 5 00am	Wheeling	5 00
91	5 30	Bellaire	4 00
101	7 00	Moundsville	5 00
103	8 00	Powhattan	2 00
117	9 00	Clarington	1 00
126	10 00	Bearsville	Saturd'y 12 00pm
128	10 30	New Martinsville	11 30
131	11 00	Sardis	11 30
137	11 30	Sistersville	10 00
142	12 00 m	Matamoras	9 00
149	1 00pm	Raven Rock	8 00
154	1 30	St. Mary's and Newport	7 00
164	2 30	Wave ly	6 00
171	3 00	Marietta	4 00
185	5 00	Parkersburg	1 00
191	7 00	Hockingport	10 00am
201	7 30	Belleville and Reedville	8 00
208	8 00	Long Bottom	8 00
214	9 00	Portland	5 00
218	9 30	Ravenswood	5 00
229	10 30	Millwood	1 00
233	11 00	Letart	12 00pm
239	12 00	Racine	Friday. 10 00
243	Thursd'y12 30am	Syracuse	9 00
247	1 00	Pomeroy and Middleport	8 00
254	2 00	Cheshire	7 00
262	2 30	Point Pleasant	5 00
266	2 50	Gallipolis	4 00
269	5 00	Brighton	2 00
275	6 00	Leon	1 00
283	7 30	Buffalo	12 00 m
293	9 30	Red Wing and Winifrede	9 00am
300	10 30	Raymond City	8 00
306	12 00 m	St. Albans	7 00
318	3 00pm	CHARLESTON	5 00

— See the other Side. —

Built from the Steamer *Capitol City* in 1893, the *Columbia* ran in the Charleston-Gallipolis-Racine trade. The *Columbia*, *Mountaineer*, *T. D. Dale*, *Lexington* and *Estola* were organized into the Kanawha Navigation Co. in 1899. Sold to the Charleston-Gallipolis Packet Company in 1901 and then to the Montgomery-Gallipolis Packet Company in 1902. Sank in 1908 while towing a showboat.

The famous "Red House Chute" as drawn by Captain Jesse P. Hughes showing old channel and dikes.

A "Man For All Seasons," Captain Hughes was a licensed pilot, a talented artist, an accomplished photographer and a meticulous note keeper. He spent a great part of his river career on the Kanawha River.

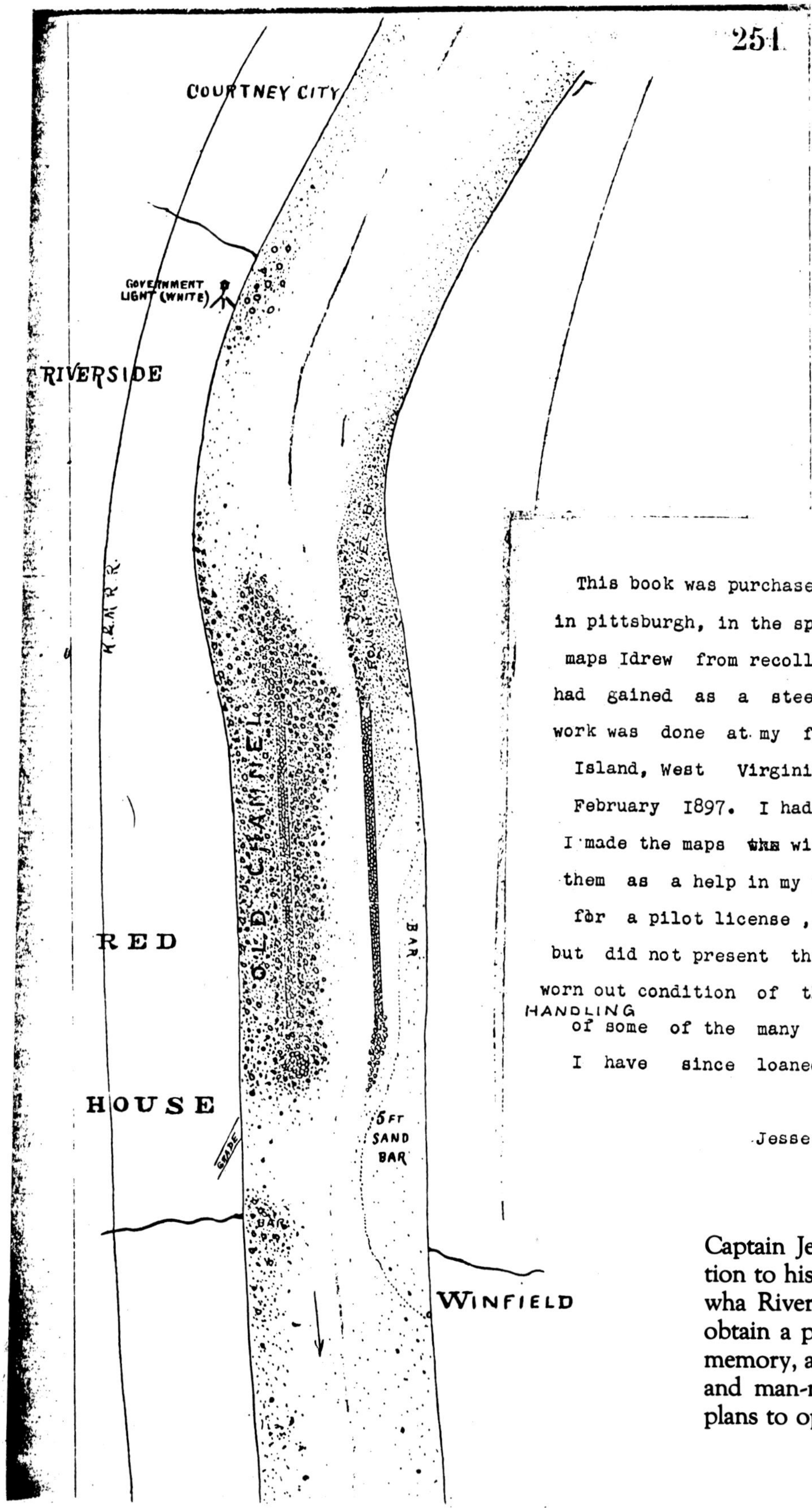

254

COURTNEY CITY

GOVERNMENT LIGHT (WHITE)

RIVERSIDE

K & M RR

OLD CHANNEL

TOUGH GRAVEL BAR

RED

HOUSE

GRADE

BAR

5 FT SAND BAR

WINFIELD

This book was purchased at Weldon's Book store in pittsburgh, in the spring of 1896. These maps I drew from recollection and knowledge I had gained as a steersman at that time . The work was done at my fathers home in Willow Island, West Virginia, during January and February 1897. I had no data for referance. I made the maps the with the thought of using them as a help in my prospective examination for a pilot license , which I took in June 1897 but did not present them at the time. The worn out condition of the book is due to rough HANDLING of some of the many different persons to whom I have since loaned it.

Jesse P Hughes.

Captain Jesse P. Hughes' typed introduction to his hand drawn maps of the Kanawha River. A part of the examination to obtain a pilot's license was to draw from memory, all the river with all of its natural and man-made features for the miles he plans to operate on.

List of stern and side-wheel boats plying on the Great Kanawha River, West Virginia.

Name of boat.	Character.	Length.	Breadth.	Depth.	Tonnage.
		Feet.	*Feet.*	*Feet.*	
Bee	U. S. towboat	120	22	3.2	85
Mascot *a*	U. S. launch	61	8.1	3.4	7
Goldenrod	U. S. light-house tender	150	26.5	3.7	143.58
W. F. Nesbit	Packet	200	35	6.1	576.86
Kanawha	....do	185	35	4	429.07
Henry M. Stanley	....do	180	32.4	5.5	293.71
Urania	....do	160	28	5	213.09
Columbia	....do	156	24.2	4	197.96
H. K. Bedford	....do	149	27.6	4	139.68
Speedwell	....do	140	25	4	149.40
Ruth	....do	136.5	24.5	4.4	131.78
Kanawha Belle	....do	128	24.2	4	133.50
Mountaineer	....do	122	20.2	4	110.52
T. D. Dale	....do	111.6	19.7	3.2	85.77
Ida Smith	....do	111.6	17.9	2.6	44.14
Sip Bays	....do	105.5	14.6	1.9	24.12
Claribell	....do	100	18.8	2	71.48
Neptune	....do	62.6	12	2.2	19.83
Genevieve	....do	59.9	11.6	2.6	12.37
E. R. Andrews	Towboat	165	32.5	5.2	351.07
Otto Marmet	....do	149.5	24	4.8	135.20
Convoy	....do	146	26.5	3.7	170.53
William Ernst	....do	140	25.2	4	197.64
Coal Bluff	....do	136	24.	4.4	162.14
Mount Clare	....do	134.5	25.8	4.8	191.36
D. T. Lane	....do	129.6	24.1	4	146.94
G. W. Moredock	....do	126.5	25.4	3.2	148.75
Gate City	....do	125	25.7	4.5	109.44
Lyda	....do	120	21.4	3.4	107.90
Jessie	....do	120	20	3.4	68.47
Annie L	....do	115.8	20.3	3.1	114.69
J. M. Bowell	....do	115	23	3.8	107.91
Geo. Matheson	....do	112	22	4	124.06
W. B. Calderwood	....do	112	24.5	4.6	85.55
Alex. Martin	....do	109.4	20	3.2	57.39
Reba Reeves	....do	107	22	3.4	63.11
Ada V	....do	82	13.6	2.6	23.38
Stella	....do	76	16.3	2.5	20.86
G. T. Thayer	....do	49	9.3	2.2	7.95
Troubadour	Show boat	93.4	18	3	61.37
Billy Martin *a*	Pump and harbor boat	89	14.3	4	28.15
Iron Duke *a*	....do	88	13.5	3.7	30.63
Madge *a*	Pleasure boat	66.5	10.5	4	9.90
Veva *a*	....do	26	6	3.5	3
Ruth *a*	....do	25	5	4	2

a Screw propeller.

Corps of Engineers report listing commodities shipped and steamboats operating on the Kanawha River for 1897. Note the number of packets and the number of passengers passing through each of the locks.

Tonnage of the Great Kanawha River for the calendar year ending December 31, 1897.

Articles.		Quantity.	Tonnage.
Coal	bushels	16,267,000	650,680
Timber	feet B. M.	17,344,000	28,906
Staves, oak	number	25,000	187
Bark and wood for tanning	cords	5,550	10,545
Hoop poles	number	344,000	860
Railroad ties, oak	do	762,000	88,583
Shingles	do	2,101,000	315
Bricks	do	173,500	434
Salt	barrels	1,660	232
Merchandise and produce in steamboats			51,260
Total			832,002

Commerce passing each of the seven finished locks and dams in Great Kanawha River, West Virginia, during the calendar year ending December 31, 1897.

Articles.	Lock No. 2.	Lock No. 3.	Lock No. 4.	Lock No. 5.	Lock No. 6.	Lock No. 7.	Lock No. 8.
Coal .... bushels	1,566,000	2,274,500	5,038,200	6,961,900	11,098,000	11,301,600	15,739,000
Coke .... tons	2,500	2,500	2,500	2,500	2,500	2,500	2,500
Lumber, etc .... feet	147,500	1,791,800	1,741,400	1,886,560	5,055,350	3,599,750	5,318,000
Shingles .... number	66,000	145,000	669,750	1,032,250	40,000	39,300	10,000
Bricks .... do	10,600	41,300	36,720	42,490	131,000	11,000	14,200
Miscellaneous freight..tons	2,862	5,827	10,188	12,173	18,485	17,365	19,210
Steamboats ...... number	1,456	1,560	1,668	1,763	1,823	1,772	1,938
Coal barges .... do	238	360	750	1,283	1,556	1,707	2,292
Other craft .... do	34	93	84	119	130	175	214
Passengers .... do	6,303	10,077	16,605	25,678	27,537	15,760	11,456
Salt .... barrels	239	525	505	1,277	30,950	39,225	514,900
Railroad ties .....number					19,450	39,225	50
Hoop poles .... do						19,450	
Bark .... cords					125	200	
Lockages .... number	1,489	1,653	1,023	1,149	1,125	881	1,167

— 81 —

GORDON C. GREENE,
Master.

CHAS. STALDER,
Purser.

Leaves Pittsburg,
Friday at 4 P. M.

Leaves Charleston,
Monday at Midnight.

STEAMER **GREENWOOD.**

ON BOARD, *May 9th* 1901.

Steamer *Greenwood* landed at the Pt. Pleasant, W. Va. wharfboat while the steamer *Kanawha* waits to land.

The "goose that laid the golden egg" for the Greene Line Steamboat Company is how Captain Gordon C. Greene described the steamer *Greenwood.*

Built at Parkersburg, W. Va. in 1898, the *Greenwood* originally ran in the Pittsburgh-Parkersburg trade but was soon extended to include the Kanawha River. Later ran in the Cincinnati-Pomeroy-Charleston trade. Retired in 1925.

Steamer *H. K. Bedford* as she looked when purchased by Captain Greene.

In the spring of 1890, Captain Gordon C. Greene went to Nashville to buy a steamboat. He was trying to decide between the *H. K. Bedford* and the *Matt F. Allen.* While sitting on the levee, when he began a conversation with an out of work Negro roustabout.

"So you have worked on both these boats?"

"Yas, Suh, both of them."

"Which one was the best?"

"De *Allen* got class and she can whup de *Bedford* with no signifyin'. But de *Bedford* is come 'n go; she allus come 'n go just d' same. An' dat's about it, Mr. Bossman."

Captian Greene bought the *Bedford* and started the Green Line Steamers. The *H. K. Bedford* began operations on the Kanawha in 1896.

Stuck on a sandbar in the Kanawha River at Buffalo, summer 1896. The texas had been added to increase stateroom space without losing a trip.

CHARLESTON, CEDAR GROVE, CANNELTON AND MONTGOMERY DAILY PACKET.

Our Motto: "Live and Let Live."

E. O. CALVERT,............................MASTER.
J. F. CALVERT,.............................CLERK.

M *T. J. Paxton*   AUG 13 1896

To Str, **KANAWHA BELLE**, Dr.

All towing done and live stock shipped at owner's risk.

Leaves CHARLESTON,......at 9:30 A. M.
Leaves CANNELTON,......at 4:00 P. M.

In no case whatever will the boat be responsible for freight after she leaves the landing.

MARKS.   TO FREIGHT *2 Pkgs Mdse*   FREIGHT CHARGES: *25*   AMOUNT.

RECEIVED PAYMENT,

Clerk.

Steamer *Kanawha Belle* (2nd) shown in the lock chamber at one of the old lock and dams on the Kanawha.

Built by the Calvert family from the Steamer *Bellaire* after she burned in 1892, the *Kanawha Belle* ran daily between Charleston and Montgomery with her sister boat, *Calvert*.

On the night of December 19, 1901 the *Kanawha Belle* was lost in a tragic accident at lock No. 3 at Riverside.

THE CHARLESTON DAILY MAIL

—FORMERLY THE MAIL-TRIBUNE—

VOLUME XVII. NO. 53 CHARLESTON, WEST VIRGINIA, FRIDAY MORNING, DECEMBER 20, 1901. THREE CEN

STRAIGHT OVER THE DAM GOES THE KANAWHA BELLE

And the Well Known and Popular Steamer Lies a Total Wreck at the Bottom Below---Singular Fatality to the Steamer of the Calvert Line at Lock Three Last Evening---Eight Lives Lost and One Serious Injury.

A passenger and freight boat, the Kanawha Belle, wrecked and sunk, eight colored deck hands drowned, a passenger dead from fright, and a colored porter with his hip dislocated is the result of a disaster on the Kanawha river Thursday evening at Lock No. 3, about twenty miles above the city. The casualty list is as follows:

LEN MARTIN, Alden City, died of fright.

The Calvert reached this city last night shortly after 10 o'clock and brought us full particulars of the disaster as can be obtained at this time. J. F. Calvert, who had charge of the Kanawha Belle, was seen by the Daily Mail last night. He said he did not know how the accident occurred, it all came so suddenly, but the one that for some reason the boat had become unmanageable. He was bruised about the arms, hands and legs.

from fright, G. T. Lanham and son, of Handley, and a boy by the name of Johnson, also from Handley. They all escaped. The wonder was how the fireman and the engineer, who were down so close to the water line made their escape. As soon as they heard the crash that told them something was wrong, they ran to the outer rail and climbed rapidly up the side of the boat until they reached the very top, landing on the roof. J. F. Calvert, ...

up the side of the boat through the rising water all around them. Fireman Woodrum, after he reached the top of the boat helped to rescue Mr. Martin, whom they pulled through a hole in the roof.

All those who were on the Calvert last night, who had been in the wreck, showed the strain of having gone through so trying an experience.

Captain E. W. Calvert, the regular captain, was not on the ...

The *Kanawha Belle* had left Charleston at 9:30 a.m. on December 19, 1901 on her usual run upstream to Montgomery. As the trip progressed, the cold day became colder and snowy.

Pilot J. H. "Musty" Snyder had just locked through lock No. 3 before being relieved by pilot Mills Calvert to have supper. While "Musty" ate, the *Belle* continued upstream making her regular landings.

Unknown to "Musty" the *Belle* made her last landing at Handley and did not go on up to Montgomery because there were no passengers or freight on board for there. The *Belle* was now heading downstream.

When "Musty" returned to the pilothouse after supper he thought the boat was still heading upstream and in the blinding snow storm steered the boat downstream toward lock and dam No. 3.

In the confusion, the *Belle* went over the dam killing eight roustabouts and completely wrecking the boat. A passenger on the boat later died with the rest of the passengers and crew being rescued by the *Kanawha Belle*'s sister boat *Calvert* that was waiting to lock up through lock No. 3 on her return trip to Montgomery from Charleston.

THOMAS-SCHOLZ COAL CO.,
MINERS AND SHIPPERS OF
STEAM AND DOMESTIC COALS.
ALL SIZES CAREFULLY PREPARED.

J. R. THOMAS, PRES. AND TREAS.
C. SCHOLZ, SEC'Y AND MANAGER.

RIVER OR RAIL SHIPMENTS.
Shipments Subject to Labor Troubles, Transportation Facilities and Other Causes Beyond Our Control.
TELEGRAPH and EXPRESS OFFICE, CEDAR GROVE, W. VA.

Mammoth, Kanawha Co., W. Va., DEC 20 1901

U S Local Inspectors
Gentlemen O
Kanawha Belle went over Dam #3 Eight Drowned one Died afterward Passenger will write you later
Yours &c
E A Calvert

Captain E. O. Calvert's brief telegraph message to the U.S. Steamboat Inspectors informing them of *Kanawha Belle*'s accident and the deaths.

Steamer *Calvert* at the wreck of the *Kanawha Belle*.

The *Calvert* had originally been named *Estola* when built at Charleston, W. Va. in 1899. Renamed in 1901, the *Calvert* was owned by J.F., M.A. and M.W. Calvert of Charleston. She was later sold, renamed *Sophia M. Gardner* and ended her career towing the showboat *Cotton Blossom*.

Captain E. O. Clavert's letter to the U. S. Steamboat Inspectors requesting to have his license renewed because his were lost in the *Kanawha Belle* disaster.

Owned by the Carr Milling Co., the *Speedwell* was built in 1897 for Kanawha River trades. Sold in 1902 and her name changed to *Helen M. Gould.*

People's Transportation Company, Between Gallipolis, Ohio, and Charleston, W. Va.

Leaves CHARLESTON Every Monday, Wednesday and Friday at 6:00 a. m. Eastern Time.
Leaves GALLIPOLIS Every Tuesday, Thursday and Saturday at 5 :a. m. Central Time.

Buffalo Nov 14 1900

M *R. G. Fife*

R. E. GACHES, MASTER.
JOHN DOUGLASS, CLERK.

To Steamer **SPEEDWELL**, Dr.,

MARKS.	TO FREIGHT ON.	FREIGHT.	CHARGES.	AMOUNT.
	1 Pkg ostgs	25		

REGULAR CHARLESTON, MONTGOMERY AND MT. CARBON DAILY PACKET.

Lv. Charleston every Morning at 8 a. m.
Lv. Mt. Carbon every Evening at 3:30 p. m.

190

To Steamer **ESTOLA** Dr.

All Towing Done and Live Stock Shipped at Owner's Risk. In no case will this Boat be responsible for Freight after she leaves the landing.

MARKS.	TO FREIGHT ON.	FREIGHT.	CHARGES.	AMOUNT.
	Box Hair			

REGULAR WINFIELD, POCA, St. ALBANS and CHARLESTON DAILY PACKET.

Lv. Charleston Every Evening at 8 p. m.
Lv. Winfield Every Morning at 5:30 a. m.
Daily Except Sunday.

Morgans 3/24 1902

M *John Morgan*

To Steamer **T. D. DALE,** Dr.

In no Case Will This Boat be Responsible for Freight After She Leaves the Landing.

AUSTIN BEAVER, MASTER.

MARKS	TO FREIGHT ON	FREIGHT	CHARGES	AMOUNT
2	1 Sheet do heston T Belt	25		

RECEIVED PAYMENT,

CLERK

Built and operated on the Ohio River, the *T. D. Dale* was sold in the late 1890s to run on the Kanawha River. Dismantled in 1902.

Built in 1898 at Pt. Pleasant, W. Va., the *Neva* ran daily, except Sunday, Gallipolis-Buffalo. This trade was later extended to Winfield.

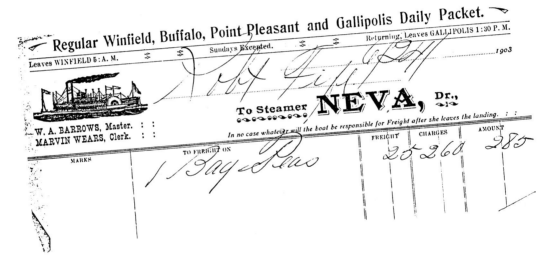

The *Neva* burned at Buffalo on Saturday, September 24, 1904 at 11:00 a.m. She had steam up when the fire started and as the flames consumed the boat her whistle blew and blew. Speculations for the whistle blowing range from the valve being tied down to a timber falling on the valve.

OHIO AND GREAT KANAWHA RIVER PACKET COMPANY

STR. KANAWHA

ON BOARD. 190____

Built at Ironton, Ohio in 1896 for the Pittsburgh-Charleston trade, the *Kanawha* was to spend the most of the next twenty years doing this Ohio-Kanawha Rivers trade. The *Kanawha* was to meet her tragic end in 1916 running from Pittsburgh to Charleston as related at the end of this chapter.

Steamer *Kanawha* waits to land at Pt. Pleasant wharf-boat while the *Greenwood* makes ready to leave.

The *Tacoma* possibly holds the record for a continuously operating packet for not having a name change or alteration in appearance for her entire 39-year career. Built in 1883 for the Ohio River Packet Co., the *Tacoma* was sold in 1904 to run in the Cincinnati-Pomeroy-Charleston trade. She burned in 1922 while still in this trade.

Head clerk Dave Scatterday and others in the *Tacoma's* cabin. Scatterday became the *Tacoma's* clerk in 1896 and was still her clerk in 1915.

The *Tacoma* in lock chamber at old Lock No. 9, Kanawha River upbound for Charleston, 1916.

Steamer *Valley Belle* as she appeared while operating as a packet. Built in 1883, she ran in the Muskingum and upper Ohio Rivers trade before being sold in 1914 to the upper Kanawha River trade teamed with the *Helen Lane*. Rebuilt twice while a packet, she was converted to a towboat in 1917.

She later towed Billy Bryant's showboat before being dismantled in 1943. The *Valley Belle* ran 34 years as a packet, then she was a towboat for 26 years. For a wooden hull steamboat carrying the same name, she has no peer for longevity.

This low water packet was built from the *T.D. Dale* at Pt. Pleasant in 1909 with one boiler and one smokestack. She ran in a variety of trades on the Monongahela, Ohio and Kanawha Rivers before being sold in 1921 and rebuilt into the *J. P. Davis*.

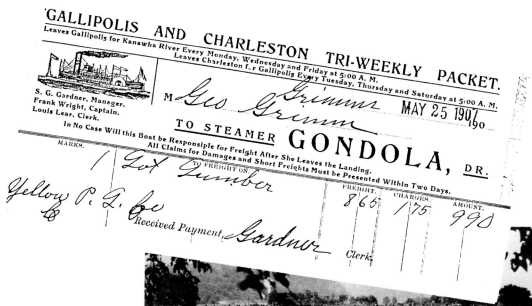

Built at Pittsburgh in 1883 and named *Gondola*, she was bought in 1887 by the Mississippi River Commission and named *Vedette*. Later sold and renamed *Gondola*, she was bought by Syl Gardner of Pt. Pleasant in 1905 to run on the Gallipolis-Charleston trade. Dismantled in 1911.

The well traveled *Leroy* was built at Levanna, Ohio in 1896 and started her career in the Wheeling-Parkersburg trade. Ran briefly on the Muskingum River, then Wheeling to Clarington on the Ohio River. She was then sold to run between Morgantown and Fairmont on the Monogahela River. Bought in 1908 to replace the *Neva* in the Winfield-Gallipolis trade on the Kanawha. Later teamed with the *Evergreen* in the Gallipolis-Charleston trade. Sold again in 1920, the *Leroy* again worked the Monogahela and upper Ohio River trades.

Steamer *Evergreen* loaded with a Sunday afternoon excursion. Packets played an important role in the social life of the valley dwellers.

When built for Captain Gordon C. Greene in 1902, the *Evergreen* ran in the Winfield-Charleston trade. Later ran in the Gallipolis-Charleston trade. Dismantled in 1916 when steamer *Chris Green* (1st) was built to replace her.

Daily packet *J.Q. Dickinson* making a landing somewhere along her Charleston-Montgomery route. Built on the hull of the side-wheel steamer *Zanetta* with the engines from the *Kanawha Belle* in 1906, the *Dickinson* was owned and operated by the Calvert Brothers of Charleston.

Steamer *J. Q. Dickinson* warehouse at Montgomery was used in later years by the packets *Helen Lane* and *Valley Belle*. From Montomery the little sternwheel gasboat *Cuba* carried light freight on upstream to Deepwater.

..... FOR PASSENGERS, FREIGHT, AND LIGHT TOWING .....

THE STEAMER CUBA

WILL LEAVE MONTGOMERY		WILL LEAVE DEEPWATER	
AT	A. M.	AT	A. M.
AT	A. M.	AT	A. M.
AT	P. M.	AT	P. M.
AT	P. M.	AT	P. M.
AT	P. M.	AT	P. M.

Pleasure parties taken out at reasonable rates. For further information, apply to

E. B. GOOSMAN,
MONTGOMERY. W. VA.

J. Q. Dickinson and *Cuba* landed at Montgomery before going their separate ways on the Kanawha.

List of steamboats plying Kanawha River, West Virginia, for the calendar year 1908.

[All stern-wheel, except as noted.]

Name of boat.		Character.	Length.	Breadth.	Depth.	Tonnage.
a Side-wheel.	*b* Screw-propeller.		*Feet.*	*Feet.*	*Feet.*	
Greenland *a*		Packet	204.4	31.9	5.4	294
Ohio		do	199.2	33.4	4.4	361
Tacoma		do	182.3	32.4	5.0	276
Kanawha		do	180.6	35.2	5.2	429
Greenwood		do	168.5	30.0	4.4	270
J. Q. Dickinson		do	135.5	24.5	5.1	143
Argand		do	132.6	24.0	5.0	96
Cricket		do	132.6	18.3	2.9	65
Chas. B. Pearce		do	132.0	33.0	4.0	130
Calvert		do	122.0	20.2	4.0	110
Leroy		do	120.5	22.4	4.2	142
Gondola		do	120.2	23.0	3.2	99
Evergreen		do	119.5	22.5	3.5	99
Neva		do	117.0	21.6	3.4	71
Genevieve		do	59.9	11.9	2.6	14
E. R. Andrews		Towboat	165.0	32.5	5.2	469
Florence Marmet		do	155.0	30.8	5.0	263
A. M. Scott *b*		do	150.9	26.0	5.8	168
Robert P. Gillham		do	149.5	31.5	4.3	158
J. T. Hatfield		do	144.5	28.8	5.6	153
J. B. Lewis		do	141.4	26.0	4.4	162
Emerson		do	140.0	26.2	4.0	192
Catherine Davis		do	135.6	26.5	4.0	334
Lucie Marmet		do	134.8	28.7	4.8	185
Crown Hill		do	132.4	26.0	4.6	366
D. T. Lane		do	129.0	24.0	4.0	146
Otto Marmet		do	128.6	25.7	4.5	135
Douglas Hall		do	127.5	27.2	4.3	122

The decline in the number of packets on the Kanawha is evident in this 1908 Corps of Engineers report. Equally notable is the large number of small gas work or pleasure boats reflecting the change to more recreation time for more people.

Name of boat.	Character.	Length.	Breadth.	Depth.	Tonnage.
		Feet.	*Feet.*	*Feet.*	
Valley Belle	Towboat	127.4	22.9	3.4	79
Vernie Mac	do	127.0	24.7	4.9	122
Mountain State	do	122.0	29.6	5.0	142
Conquest	do	121.0	23.5	3.0	209
J. M. Bowell	do	120.6	22.9	4.3	94
John W. Love	do	120.0	20.4	4.0	88
Winifrede	do	119.4	24.9	4.6	97
W. B. Calderwood	do	112.0	24.5	4.6	85
Sallie Marmet	do	109.3	20.6	4.0	51
French	do	104.8	19.9	4.0	82
Antoinette	do	100.7	19.9	3.9	54
Mary Stewart	do	100.0	24.3	3.4	77
Katie Mc	do	98.1	18.0	2.8	41
M. L. Thornton	do	73.6	14.0	2.6	26
Ada V	do	82.0	13.6	2.6	23
Monie Bauer	do	73.0	17.5	3.0	45
James Rumsey	U. S. towboat	120.0	22.0	4.3	125
Golden Rod	U. S. light-house tender	150.0	26.5	3.7	471
Mascot *a*	U. S. launch	61.0	8.0	3.7	7
Billy Martin *a*	Pump and harbor	89.0	14.3	4.0	28
Iron Duke *a*	do	88.0	13.5	3.7	30

BOATS PROPELLED BY GASOLINE.

a Screw-propeller.

Name of boat.	Character.	Length.	Breadth.	Depth.	Tonnage.
Van M	Launch				
Shamrock	do	59.3	13.3	2.7	12
Bertha *a*	do				
Amantha *a*	do				
Polly *a*	do				
Florence *a*	do				
Nellie *a*	do				
Margaret	do				
Maggie Harper	do				
Ajax *a*	do				
Borealis	do	47.0	9.0	1.4	8
Friend	do	51.5	12.0	2.3	12
Bessie Grimm *a*	do				
Good Luck *a*	do				
Ivanhoe *a*	do				
Pirate	do	44.6	10.0	2.0	8
Clarion *a*	do				
Elvira	do	66.8	9.3	2.6	14
Denver *a*	do				
Phantom *a*	do				
Archa *a*	do				
J. C. Montgomery *a*	do				
Smithey *a*	do				
Leonora	do				
Dig *a*	do				
St. Henry *a*	do				
Relief No. 1 *a*	do				
Relief No. 2 *a*	do				
Leader *a*	do				
Anna M *a*	do				
St. Albans *a*	do				
Midget *a*	do				
Sport *a*	do				
Little Chief *a*	do				
Beck *a*	do				
Kanawha Star *a*	do				
Alice *a*	do				
Dart *a*	do				
Flubaloo *a*	do				
Chas. B. Payne *a*	do				
E. L. Wilson *a*	do				
Teddie *a*	do				
Eagle *a*	do				
Little Bill	do				
Mist *a*	do				
Will H. Stone *a*	do				
Elizabeth *a*	do				
Gallipolis *a*	do				
Lizzie D *a*	do				
Cuba	do	50.0	9.6	2.5	10
J. P. Lightner	do	40.0	12.6	3.0	8

— 95 —

MRS. M. B. GREENE, Master.   SAM. MADDY, Purser.

Pittsburgh to Charleston, $5.50.   Round Trip $10.00, including meals and Berth.

GREENE LINE---NEW AND ELEGANT STEAMER

"GREENLAND"

**Only
Side
Wheel
Boat
Going
to
Pittsburgh**

BETWEEN

Wheeling, Marietta,
Parkersburg,
Pomeroy,
Point Pleasant,
Gallipolis,
Charleston and
Montgomery.

Leaves PITTSBURGH every Friday at 4 p. m.
Leaves CHARLESTON every Monday at 6 p. m.

REGULAR PITTSBURGH AND KANAWHA RIVER PACKET

For Freight and Passenger Rates apply on Board Steamboat or to S. R. Patterson & Co., 307 Water Street, Pittsburgh, Pa., or George H. Christ, Agents.   Telephone 423 Pittsburgh.

W. B DONNALLY, & CO. . . . . CHARLESTON, W. VA.

Captain Mary B. Greene directing a landing from the roof of the steamer *Greenland.* Designed and built for the Pittsburgh-Charleston trade in 1902, the *Greenland* ran most of her career in the Cincinnati-Pomeroy-Charleston trade.

The last boat operated by the Greene Line Steamers was the *Delta Queen*. In 1969 the company was sold and the *Delta Queen* still runs today (1991) in a tourist business that was pioneered by the *Greenland* with four trips from the Ohio River to the World's Fair at St. Louis in 1904.

Greenland cabin

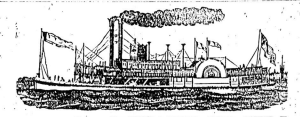
The side-wheel *Liberty* was known more for being slow rather than for her speed as the hand bill might lead the reader to believe.

Within three years after being built, the *Liberty* had been sold three times. Her third purchase was made in 1903 by the Charleston Steamboat Excurison Company but her stay on the Kanawha was brief and by 1905 she was running in the excursion business on the Monogahela River.

Photo courtesy of Ann Emich

Steamers *Greenland* and *Liberty* landed at the Charleston Riverfront circa 1903.

Bought in 1907 for the Pittsburgh-Charleston trade, the *Avalon* had begun her career in 1898 on the upper Ohio River before being taken to the Tennessee River in 1901. Her stay on the Kanawha was brief as the *Avalon* with her name being changed to *Ohio* in 1908.

Big Excursion STEAMER "OHIO"

Will Run a Moonlight Excursion

THURSDAY SEPT. 10, 1914

Will leave Charleston Wharf at 7:30 p. m. and return at 11:30 p. m. same evening. The boat carries their own orchestra. Dancing will be free.

Tickets 50 Cents---Pays All

This will give the people of Charleston an opportunity to make a trip on the finest Excursion Boat on the waters of the Mississippi River. All Fraternal Organizations and the public invited.

The boat reserves the right to reject all objectionable parties.

Returning to the Kanawha River to run excursions in 1914, the *Ohio* had originally run on this river as the steamer *Avalon* in 1907. In 1908 she was given the name *Ohio* and operated about a year on the Kanawha before being placed in the Cincinnati-Pittsburgh trade. Burned on February 2, 1916 at Parkersburg.

MANY ENJOY RIVER TRIP ON KANAWHA

Excursion on the Palatial Homer Smith Was a Gala Occasion Yesterday

With absolutely no fear of being attacked by a German submarine five hundred people, men, women and children, boarded the Homer Smith about three-thirty yesterday to enjoy a trip up the Kanawha river. The ladies of the first division of the M. E. Church, South, had chartered the boat for the afternoon trip. Many people with a Saturday half holiday made the best of it, packed their lunches, and prepared to enjoy a beautiful trip

Music sounds best on water is an old saying, perhaps from more than one point of view. However the music heard on the trip yesterday was excellent and received the applause of all on board. Miss Ingerick sang that old favorite, "O dry those tears," and Mr. Dowman, of St. Albans, sang several selections, all of which were well received. Mr. E. S. Lanhon, of Catlettsburg, was the special singer and his selections and singing proved him worthy of the name. A quartet composed of Miss Ingerick, Miss Davidson, Mr. Cupid and Mr. Petticrew entertained the passengers with some old delightful melodies.

The weather for the whole trip was delightful. The sun was just warm enough to make all feel glad that they were away from the noise and hustle of a city and wandering peacefully between the beautiful green-clad banks of the Kanawha. The calmness of the weather coaxed out many who are always afflicted with that dread disease, sea sickness. No signs of it could anywhere be seen. The boat, so spacious and well designed to meet every comfort that one might hope to enjoy, was not over crowded. People had plenty of room to promenade here and there at will.

The Homer Smith will run two excursions today leaving the wharf at 2:00 p. m. and 8:00 p. m. Due to the fact that the steamer is too wide to pass through lock five above the city, the trip today may be made down the river instead of up as planned

Sunday morning, April 18, 1915, the *Homer Smith* is locking through Lock No. 11 on the Kanawha River on her one and only trip to Charleston.

Built in 1914 by the Security Steamboat Co., a group of businessmen investors of Point Pleasant, the *Homer Smith* became a regular excursion boat at Pittsburgh. She ran "tramp" excursions in the spring all on the Ohio River. Sold in 1928 to the Pittsburgh Amusement Company who renamed her *Greater Pittsburgh*. Burned at Pittsburgh, April 1931.

Running as a ferry between Charleston and Nitro, W. Va. during the construction of a munitions plant, the *Virginia* had originally operated on the Monogahela River as the *I. C. Woodward*. Sold at a U. S. Marshall sale in August 1919 and name changed to *City of Charleston.*.

The *City of Charleston* operated briefly as an excursion boat on the Kanawha River in 1919 and 1920. Moved to Pittsburgh in 1920 to operate on the Monogahela River but could not pass under the Port Perry Bridge. Burned at Gallipolis, Ohio on May 5, 1921.

Named for both the father and oldest son of Captain Gordon C. Greene, the *Chris Greene* was the first of two boats to carry this name. Known on the river as the "*Little Chris*," she ran in the Gallipolis-Charleston trade from 1915 to 1918.

Built from equipment from the *J. Q. Dickinson* in 1915 at Dana, W. Va., the *Helen Lane* ran for three years on the Kanawha before being sold south.

The *Ruth* ran in the Pittsburgh-Charleston trade in 1896 before being moved to various Ohio River trades. She came back to the Kanawha in 1916 to again work the Pittsburgh-Charleston trade. Sank in the ice, January 1918.

Named for a storekeeper (Reuben Dunbar) at Greasy Creek, Kentucky, the *R. Dunbar* started her career on the Cumberland River in 1895. She ran on the Kanawha from 1914 until sold and named *General Crowder* in 1918.

Named for the famed World War I general, the *General Pershing* was originally named *Lora* when built in 1900. Later rebuilt, her name was changed to *Omaha* in 1908.

The *General Pershing* came to the Pittsburgh-Charleston trade in 1918 and ran there until the end of her career.

The Liberty Transit Company of Wheeling bought the *R. Dunbar* in 1918 and renamed her *General Crowder*. Ran in the Pittsburgh-Charleston trade until 1922 when extensive repairs were made and she ran on the Cincinnati-Pittsburgh trade.

STEAMER "SENATOR CORDILL"

PITTSBURGH AND CHARLESTON
Leaves PITTSBURGH Tuesday, 4:00 P. M.
Leaves CHARLESTON Thurs., 10:00 P. M.

From Pittsburgh to the foot hills of the Blue Ridge Mountains on one of the best and most suitable passenger vessels to be found on the Ohio River is the trip offered on the Steamer Senator Cordill. She easily accommodates seventy-five people. Her staterooms, all outside, are large and comfortable, well ventilated, and neatly furnished. She has extensive promenade and lounging deck space. The main cabin is wide and of massive and ornate construction, after the style of the great steamboats of long ago. The table service and cuisine are all that one could reasonably desire.

This steamer is officered by men of long and varied river experience, thoroly competent and alive to the delicate task of caring for the safety and catering to the enjoyment of tourists. In her five years' operations over the Pittsburgh-Charleston route, she has won an enviable reputation among the many hundreds who have patronized her.

The Ohio is too well known to require any attempt at description here. Of the Great Kanawha, a lesser stream, relatively little has been published. In its lower reaches, we traverse a rich agricultural country, dotted with sleepy villages. Gradually the country assumes a more rugged aspect, evergreens mantle the hillsides, and coal mining replaces farming as the chief activity. Then, as we approach the end of the route, the smoke and bustle of the suburbs of Charleston remind us strongly that we have reached not only the Capital City, but a great and thriving industrial center here in the heart of West Virginia.

STEAMER "GENERAL WOOD"

PITTSBURGH AND CHARLESTON
Leaves PITTSBURGH Tuesday, 4:00 P. M.
Leaves CHARLESTON Thur., 10:00 P. M.
(E. S. T.)

The Steamer GENERAL WOOD, originally a Southern cotton boat, was rebuilt some years ago for service on the Upper Ohio. She has since been operated between Pittsburgh and Charleston, W. Va., making a round trip each week. This boat has proven very popular with summer pleasure trippers. A large number of former patrons reserve berths early each season that they may again enjoy her spacious lounging deck, the good meals and the thousand miles of diversified scenery.

This steamer is officered by men of long and varied river experience, thoroughly competent and alive to the delicate tasks of caring for the safety and catering to the enjoyment of tourists. In her operations over the Pittsburgh-Charleston route, she has won an enviable reputation among the many hundreds who have patronized her.

The Ohio is too well known to require any attempt at description here. Of the Great Kanawha, a lesser stream, relatively little has been published. In its lower reaches, we traverse a rich agricultural region, dotted with sleepy villages. Gradually the country assumes a more rugged aspect, evergreens mantle the hillsides, and coal mining replaces farming as the chief activity. Then . . .

Both the *General Wood* and *Betsy Ann* found the Kanawha a good market for the tourist boat trade during the late 1920's.

The *General Wood* like the *Senator Cordill* was a southern cotton boat that had been brought to the upper Ohio River trade at the end of World War I. The *Wood* ran mostly in the Pittsburgh-Cincinnati trade until she was laid up at Pittsburgh in 1929.

The *Senator Cordill* was built in 1902 for the Vicksburg-Natchez trade. Bought for the Pittsburgh-Charleston trade in 1920, the *Cordill's* story is told later in this chapter.

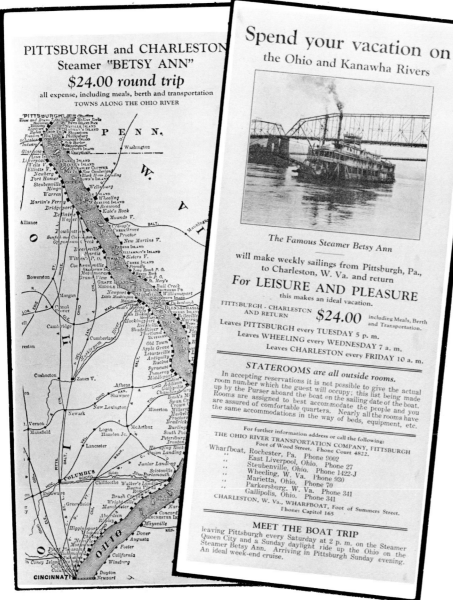

The subject of the book, *The Log of the Betsy Ann* by Captain Frederick Way, Jr., the *Betsy Ann* ran on the Kanawha in 1930.

Built in 1899 at Dubuque, Iowa, the *Betsy Ann* is best remembered for the series of steamboat races she ran with the *Chris Greene* and *Tom Greene* in 1928, 1929 and 1930 at Cincinnati.

The second *Chris Greene* was built at Charleston at the Ward Engineering Company and completed at Point Pleasant in 1925. Ran in the Cincinnati-Pomeroy-Charleston trade until 1934, then ran Cincinnati-Louisville. In 1936 all of her state rooms were removed to permit her to be used to carry automobiles. Withdrawn from service in 1947.

Steamer *Chris Greene* landed at the Charleston wharfboat in 1934. Photograph by Captain C. W. Stoll.

Named for the youngest son of Greene Line Steamers owner, Captain Gordon C. Greene, the *Tom Greene* was built at Pt. Pleasant, W. Va. in 1925. She ran as a partner with the *Chris Greene* in the Cincinnati-Pomeroy-Charleston trade. Entered the Cincinnati-Louisville trade in 1931 and ran there until 1947. Her passenger cabins removed in 1936 to make room for carrying new automobiles. Sold in 1950 to become a landing boat.

Steamer *Gordon C. Greene* making one of its many trips on the Kanawha River. Originally named *Cape Girardeau* when built in 1923, her name was changed in 1935 when acquired by the Greene Line Steamers for the company founder.

At a time when passenger boats were a rare sight on the Inland Rivers, the *Gordon C. Greene* made trips on rivers that had not seen one in years.

With Captain Tom R. Greene commanding, his mother Captain Mary B. Greene usually on board and his wife Letha and family assisting, the *Greene* was the "family boat" that was like no other that had ever operated on the Inland Rivers.

She was retired in 1952 and became a floating restaurant at a number of locations on the Ohio and Mississippi Rivers, with even a short stop at Bradenton, Florida as a tourist attraction, before sinking at St. Louis in 1967.

Steamer *Avalon* at Charleston in the 1950's.

Still running today as the very successful *Belle of Louisville*, the *Avalon* is one of the most widely traveled steamboats ever. Originally named *Idlewild* when built in 1915, this boat is remembered by many along the Kanawha for enjoyable summer afternoon and moonlight excursion in the 1940's and 50's.

West Virginia's Floating Capitol

State House, Charleston, W. Va.

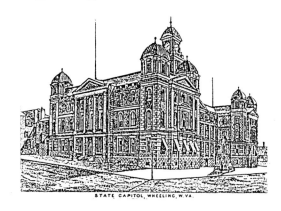

State Capitol, Wheeling, W. Va.

Between 1863 and 1885, the capitol of the new state of West Virginia was moved three times by steamboats between Wheeling on the Ohio River and Charleston on the Kanawha River.

The selection of a permanent location for the capitol of the new state that had been created in 1863 when Abraham Lincoln signed a presidential proclamation was to become a unique series of events in the state's history.

The first capitol was established at Wheeling in 1863 when the new state began operations, but the first governor made repeated requests that a permanent capitol city be selected. At this point the cities of Parkersburg, Charleston and Wheeling began vying to become the permanent capitol.

Charleston was the first city to offer the state a site and building which the Legislature voted to accept. On March 28, 1870 state officials with all state records and properties, boarded the steamer *Mountain Boy* for a trip to Charleston. Captain James Newton agreed to move the capitol to its new location stating: "I will go with cannon, music and floating flags and will consider the honor sufficient pay." As the *Mountain Boy* neared the new capitol city, the state officials were met by the steamer *Kanawha Belle* with a brass band and an enthusiastic reception committee.

However, after just five years of the capitol being in Charleston a group of citizens of Wheeling began a campaign to bring the capitol back to the Ohio River city. They offered to build the state a better Capitol building than was being used in Charleston.

On March 30, 1875, the Legislature voted to return the Capitol to Wheeling. One of the main reasons for this vote was the lack of proper hotel and communications facilities in Charleston.

Although a group of Charleston citizens were able to acquire an injunction from the Court of the Seventh Judicial District to halt this move, on May 21st the state officials boarded the steamer *Emma Graham* which took them to Parkersburg. Here the state officials transferred to the steamer *Chesapeake* to continue the trip to Wheeling.

With the officials now in Wheeling and the state records being held in Charleston by the injunction, the government of West Virginia was at a standstill. However, by September legal matters had been settled and on the 22nd the steam towboat *Iron Valley* with two barges arrived at Wheeling with the state records.

This latest move made the selection of a permanent capitol city a state-wide issue that soon required the Legislature of 1877 to direct that a state-wide election be held to allow the people of West Virginia to select the city of their choice. The election was held on August 7, 1877 with the cities of Charleston, Clarksburg and Martinsburg being choices. For some unknown reason Wheeling did not appear on the ballot. The results of the vote were: Martinsburg - 8,046, Clarksburg - 29,942, and Charleston - 41,243.

After eight years of West Virginia having a "floating capitol," Governor Henry M. Mathews proclaimed that Charleston was now the state's permanent capitol.

The final move of the state officials and records occurred on May 2, 1885 whem the steam packet *Chesapeake* along with the towboat *Belle Prince* towing the covered barge *Nick Crawley* left Wheeling for Charleston.

West Virginia's floating capitol now had a permanent home on the banks of the Great Kanawha River.

Built for the Kanawha and Gallipolis Packet Company in 1868, the *Mountain Boy* was the first steamboat used in West Virginia's "floating capitol" moves. Damaged by ice at Cincinnati during the winter of 1873, the *Mountain Boy* sank and was lost. The following June while workmen were removing the boiler from the wreck, a 40 pound catfish was found inside.

The original *Emma Graham* was built in 1855 and named for the daughter of N. W. Graham of Zanesville, Ohio. There was a second *Emma Graham* built in 1861 and lost in the ice at Antiquity, Ohio in 1872.

The third *Emma Graham* shown here, built in 1872 for the Parkersburg and Gallipolis trade, was used for one-half the capitol move from Charleston to Wheeling.

Steamer *Chesapeake* (1st) shown at Wheeling. The small caption scratched into the photograph states: "All aboard for Charleston May 2, 1885 Brown." This scene appears to have been photographed by a Mr. Brown on the day of the final move of the floating capitol.

The *Chesapeake* was also used in the second capitol move from Parkersburg to Wheeling in 1875.

MAY 4, 1885.

THE CHESAPEAKE'S ARRIVAL.

A BIG CROWD ON THE LEVEE AND SOME BUNTING ON THE HOUSES.

At precisely five minutes past six o'clock last night the Chesapeake, bearing the State officers, rounded the bend in the Kanawha, three miles below town. A mile behind her came the Belle Prince towing a model barge, in which were stored away the effects of the State Government. It was fully half an hour after the Chesapeake hove in sight before she reached the lower wharfboat, by which time the buildings along the river began to display a good deal of bunting. She carried a number of flags, and was crowded with passengers. Upon landing, the State officers were met by a large number of citizens. Gov. Wilson went immediately to his residence on Capitol street, and the other officers went down to the St. Albert.

On board the Chesapeake were: Governor E. W. Wilson and Private Secretary John Howard; Secretary of State Henry S. Walker, Chief Clerk J. B. Floyd, Clerk J. M. Scroggins and Messenger Marshall White; Auditor Patrick Duffey, Land Clerk W. A. Cracraft, and Clerks W. P. Adams, Hill Marshall, B. H. Oxley and F. B. Dailey; Superintendent of Schools B. M. Morgan, Clerk J. D. Cork; Treasurer W. T. Thompson, Clerk Robert Herndon, and lastly, Janitor W. B. Carder. Judge Jackson boarded the boat at Parkersburg.

A few minutes after the arrival of the Chesapeake the Belle Prince passed the shoals and came rapidly toward the upper wharf boat with the model barge, on the bow end of which was a cannon. This was fired several times before the boat landed. When the Prince cleared the shoals she began to whistle. At the same time a freight train on the Chesapeake & Ohio Railroad joined in, followed a few minutes later by the ferry boat, City of Charleston, the Chancellor and the Handy, which on account of a lack of steam, contributed a deep bass. By this time the crowd had increased to a thousand people at least. They continued on the levee long after the boat had landed.

There was no special demonstrations, a number of citizens, at a public meeting decided some time ago that such a thing would be unnecessary. Besides the persons mentioned above there were many people on the Chesapeake who came along for the pleasure of the trip.

Built in 1879 by Captain Bill Prince of Wheeling, the engines used on the *Belle Prince* came from the towboat *Iron Valley* which had been used in the second move of the "floating capitol" from Charleston to Wheeling. These same engines had originally been used on the Steamer *Island Packet* built in 1846. They were later used at the Crawford's flour mill at Bridgeport, Ohio until 1871 when they were placed on the *Iron Valley*.

Completed in 1932, the last permanent capitol for the state of West Virginia stands facing the Kanawha River. A feature of the capitol complex design is a landing on the river with steps leading to the front of the capitol.

Tragedy in the night—the wreck of the *Kanawha*

On January 5, 1916 the steam packet *Kanawha* sank in the Ohio River with a loss of 16 lives. The second clerk on the *Kanawha* was Fred M. Hoyt who survived the wreck and later wrote a vivid account of his memory of the tragedy. What follows is the story of the sinking of the *Kanawha* based on Fred Hoyt's original writing.

The steamer *Kanawha* left Pittsburgh just before dark on the evening of January 4, 1916. She had recently been overhauled at the Parkersburg Docks and the passengers and crew had no cause to fear that the boat was not equal to the task of completing her regular trip safely to Charleston. The pilots, engineers and mates were all well qualified and mature men. Fred Hoyt had made 130 round trips between Pittsburgh and Charleston over a period of three years. Even though the Ohio River presented a foreboding scene running high and fast Hoyt felt confident that this would be another routine trip. For rea-

sons unknown a big metal lifeboat had been removed from the boat a few weeks prior to Janaury 4th and the packet was now running without all of its usual lifesaving apparatus.

After steaming through the frigid night for 172 miles the *Kanawha* reached Marietta, Ohio on a blustery midwinters day and there fate would set into motion the first of a series of events that would eventually lead to the end of the *Kanawha*.

Henry Best owned the wharfboat at Marietta and he wanted two barrels of lubricating oil delivered to the landing at Little Hocking, Ohio. He declared that this was a rush order and had to be delivered. Captain Brady Berry had protested to Henry that the stop at Little Hocking would be difficult and dangerous especially with the high wind and the construction of Lock 19 opposite the village. Best was adamant, however and Berry did not argue further.

Fred Hoyt looked out on the Marietta Landing and saw his mother waiting to see him for a few minutes. He quickly reached her side and as they talked she spoke of her concern for her son and her premonition of an impending disaster unless Captain Berry tied the *Kanawha* up.

Fred Hoyt looked out across the river and understood his mother's concern. There were heavy swells running and the river was at a 30-foot stage. For a moment he thought about taking his mother's advice and then decided that she was just overly concerned. Bidding her a reluctant farewell he reboarded the packet and they headed downstream to Parkersburg.

Upon arriving at Parkersburg, Tom Sams, the cook, walked down the landing gangway and headed for the B & O Train Depot. He had told Captain Berry that he was frankly scared and just couldn't go on.

Fred Hoyt knew a Mrs. Fitzpatrick and her six-year-old son were scheduled to leave the boat at Lee Creek near Belleville, West Virginia, but he realized that the low bottom at Lee Creek would be flooded and she would have to get off at Belleville or even Reedsville, Ohio. He suggested to Mrs. Fitzpatrick that it might be advisable for she and her son to spend the night in Parkersburg and take the morning train home. Mrs. Fitzpatrick declined. A fateful decision on a fateful day for within a few hours she and her son would be among the victims.

From Parkersburg to Little Hocking required less than an hour and by 7:00 p.m. the graceful vessel had landed the fateful two barrels of oil and was trying to get back into the main stream. The *Kanawha* was known for her good handling but the combination of the swift current and the high wind was just too much for her—in a moment she was broadside to the waves and Captain Berry had to try a difficult manuever to bring her back on course. The river was so high that Lock 19 was completely submerged but that in itself was not a problem. The light draft packet could have safely run across the lock walls but the barely submerged light towers on each side of the lock were another matter.

At 7:20 p.m. in the pitch dark as Captain Berry struggled to "right" the boat, the *Kanawha* smashed into the lower tower. Fred Hoyt had just started for the Texas deck and was talking to Lloyd Gee, a steward when the collision occurred. Both men were nearly thrown from their feet and Hoyt remarked: "Lloyd, I fear she won't stand that!"

The tower had burst a fearful hole in the starboard side of the wooden hull just forward of the boilers. Hoyt raced out to the forward boiler deck and felt the boat tilt crazily as if to capsize. He looked back toward the ladies cabin and saw four or five women.

He considered rushing back to advise them to leave the cabin and take position at the guard rails. At that moment the generator was drowned out and the lights went off. In the awful darkness Hoyt jumped over the port rail and slid down the bull rails as the boat steadied herself for a moment.

The young clerk felt hot steam sweeping over him as the furnaces died out and then ice water swirling above his knees. Realizing that his only hope was to get higher up on the boat he climbed onto the boiler deck rail and gained a handhold on the edge of the roof. Two crewmen dragged him up to a narrow part that was not submerged. The group of five men gathered there suddenly realized that the *Kanawha*, although sunk to her roof, was still afloat. Hoyt later surmised that it was probably the thousands of empty egg crates and chicken coops in the hold that gave the boat bouyancy. By this time most everyone trapped in the lower areas of the boat had drowned. Many of them had no doubt been trapped in their staterooms by jammed doors as the twisting hull distorted the frames.

The crew and surviving passengers were crowded around the one available yawl abreast of the pilothouse. The other lifeboat had been fouled and sunk on the opposite side. Hoyt's thoughts went back to the big metal lifeboat that had been left in Pittsburgh and he bitterly remembered his mother's pleas to leave the packet at Marietta.

No one had managed to save a light of any kind and the sheer terror of this situation defys the imagination. Later powerful criticism was directed at the rank and file of the *Kanawha* crew who apparently saved themselves without regard to passengers as many of them were the first ashore.

Hoyt and his companions felt new terror grip them when the hull shuddered and jolted as she ran aground on the rock dike at the head of Newberry Island. The wreck of the *Kanawha* had swiftly covered the two miles from Lock 19 and as she paused on the dike one of the hero's of the tragedy arrived on the scene.

Harold B. Wright, a young Lock 19 employee, had immediately set out after the *Kanawha* in a big U.S. Corps of Engineers yawl. He took into shore two or more loads of survivors and left Hoyt and the others with a lantern which gave them courage. Hoyt heard one of his companions commence to curse and pray. The young man that lost his nerve that night survived and went on to become a local politician in Mason County, West Virginia. Harold B. Wright was to later become a riverboat captain and retire from the river in the 1980's.

While awaiting their turn in the lifeboat, Hoyt and the others could feel the hull grinding on the rocks under the force of the thousands of tons of rushing water. The miserable group was about to face the most incredible and heart stopping moment of that tragic night.

Suddenly, with a sickening lurch, the hull began to capsize completely. These five men had to somehow crawl around the boat from their perch on the roof as the packet rolled over to a new place of safety on the bottom of the hull. With precision born of the fear of death they backed down the stationaries and after the boat had finished her roll they were still five in number and without a scratch.

This "turn turtle" motion had wrenched the boilers free and they were later found at the foot of Newberry Island.

Mercifully the wind slacked off and a mild rain began. It was two miles to Mustapha Island which was to be the last resting place of the *Kanawha*. Hoyt could feel the hog chains dragging along the bottom and several sharp lurches nearly dislodged him. At the head of Mustapha Island, at long last, Hoyt and several others were taken aboard the packets lifeboat and they made shore.

The broken remains of the *Kanawha* drifted on with two men still clinging to the hull, Captain Berry and an old cabin boy. They were saved when the wreck went aground for the last time. It was 9:15 p.m.—two short hours since the disaster began.

The B & O Railroad ran a special train from Parkersburg to pick up survivors strung out along the shore.

Hoyt and others took refuge in a small cottage where they warmed up in front of a roaring fire. To him it seemed a "luxury lodge" and he soon was able to send a wire to his mother in Marietta to say that he had survived. Movie theatres in Marietta had already begun flashing news on the screens that the *Kanawha* had sunk.

As so often happens after such a tragic event, the unexplainable is explained by superstitions or become the basis for the beginning of new superstitions. Prior to the final trip of the *Kanawha*, while repairs were being made to the smokestacks, the spreader-bar with its decorative star was removed. When it was replaced, the star was upside down and this is the way it was on that last trip when the *Kanawha* sank and turned bottom up.

The Lady From Dixie

The *Senator Cordill* operated for 32 years, from 1902 to 1934 through the twilight years of the steam packet era.

She was built to high standards in the classic style of the golden age of steamboating for Mississippi River service between the cities of Vicksburg and Natchez in the heart of Dixie.

Ordered especially for that trade, she was built by the Howard Yard of Jeffersonville, Indiana at a near record cost. Her lines were reminiscent of the legendary packets one always thinks of when the word "steamboat" is pronounced. Plenty of attention to detail, to the little things that made a boat special—a tall pilothouse and lots of ginger-bread trim.

She was noted for keeping her schedule and it was said that Natchez churchgoers timed the parsons sermon by the noon departure whistle of the *Cordill*.

For nearly twenty years she plied the waters of "Big Muddy" until July 1920 when she was sold to a group of investors who sent her north into the upper Ohio River trade.

Pittsburgh it seems had an insatiable appetite for fresh eggs. The railroads were rough and the *Cordill* was eminently suited to deliver her delicate cargo with a minimum of breakage. Not very glamorous to be sure, but nonetheless honest work for a grand old boat that the modern era was fast leaving behind. The *Cordill* or "Caw-dell" as

Senator Cordill cabin with its wooden turned gloss white pendants with gold-leaf tips.

she was commonly known would sometimes carry along with the usual passengers and freight, up to 6,000 cases—or over one million eggs to the breakfast tables of the "Steel City."

Her melodious 3 chime Lunkenheimer whistle soon became familiar along the banks of the Great Kanawha as she went about her business 6 days a week between Charleston and Pittsburgh. Unlike the leisurely schedule of a mere 222 miles per week on the Mississippi, she now covered 655 miles a week on the Kanawha and Ohio with only Monday to rest and have her boilers cleaned at Point Pleasant.

Business was good on the Kanawha, so good in fact that in 1924 she was drydocked and 23 feet was added to the forward part of her hull for increased cargo space. This added to the her graceful good looks, although it proved to be more of a job than anticipated.

In 1926, "Lady Luck" seemed to turn her back on the *Cordill* when she "hooked a snag" near Lock 7 on the Kanawha not far from St. Albans. Down she went as the result of the 20 foot gash. Hardly anything looks so forelorn as a steamboat half under water. Careful work floated her, but less than a year later she was again embarrassed, but this time within the clear view of the entire population of Charleston.

The Shippers' Packet Co.

Consignee _M. M. Mullen. C._   Pksty .... NOV 16 1926 92

Shipper _C._   Leaves Pittsburgh Tuesday 4:00 P. M.

From _Eaton C. W. Co._   Leaves Charleston Friday 4:00 A. M.

M. O. Irwin, Master
Clyde Packard, Purser   **TO STEAMER** **Senator Cordill** DR.

MARKS	TO FREIGHT ON	WT.	RATE	FREIGHT	CHARGES	AMOUNT
1	Co Candy	1.38	43	60	11	71

Star Printing Co., Ravenswood, W. Va.

On Friday morning March 11, 1927 the *Cordill* had just departed the Charleston landing and was making her way past the mouth of Elk river on a good flow of water when somehow she got crossed up in the swift "Elk Chute" (water coming out of the Elk River into the Kanawha River), and before Captain Jesse Patchell could do anything, she was fast aground on a high rock bar. People came from miles around to witness this indignity and it was feared for a while that her hull would be smashed. Soon help arrived in the form of the towboats *Robert P. Gillham* and *W. C. Mitchell* who attached their heaviest lines to the grounded *Cordill* in an attempt to pull her free. After much ferocious thrashing of the water even these two powerful boats were defeated as the huge ropes snapped one by one.

For over two weeks the great craft sat ignominiously on the bar, twisted at an odd angle, her paddle wheel high above the water.

It wasn't until April 2nd, mercifully the day after "April Fools," that enough rain fell to float the *Cordill* off her perch.

Misfortune began to haunt this graying "Lady of the South" as various accidents befell her. Early in 1928 her throttle burst like an artillery shell and killed two of her veteran engineers along with a boilermaker from Gallipolis. The damage was slight however and in the midsummer of 1929 she commenced a new role under ownership of the Ohio River Transportation Co. in the Pittsburgh to Cincinnati trade.

The "Roaring Twenties" had just about played out and the free spending prosperity that could keep an aging Mississippi River "Queen" going would soon end.

MARCH 11, 1927   24 PAGES

CORDILL HITS ROCK, STICKS

River Packet in Danger of Breaking Up at South Charleston Bridge; Rudder Broken; Towboat Hurriedly Summoned to Scene

The "Senator Cordill" river packet from Pittsburgh, was still in danger of being broken up on the chute wall near the South Charleston bridge on the Kanawha river this afternoon, despite the efforts of a tow boat to pull it out into deep water.

The "Robert P. Gillam," one of the largest tow boats on the Kanawha, was assigned the task of dislodging the "Senator Cordill." After anchoring to a nearby island, the tow crew began operating a wheel belted with rope attached to the prow of the stranded packet.

The "Senator Cordill," three-decker river packet operating between Charleston and Pittsburgh, Pa., went on the rocks at the bend of the Kanawha river east of the South Charleston bridge at 9:30 o'clock this morning.

— 121 —

Steam towboat *Robert P. Gillham* works her tow into Lock No. 7 while the *Cordill* sits forlorn on the river bottom creating a problem for boats approaching the lock.

Re-floating the *Cordill* to permit safe access to Lock No. 7 became a priority for the U.S. Army Corps of Engineers.

The innovative steam propeller towboat *James Rumsey* is shown assisting the Corps dredge *Addison* begin efforts to raise the *Cordill*.

The strange looking building to the far left is the old Nitro Water Works. A visit to the area about 1½ miles below the St. Albans bridge will provide a modern view of this scene.

The towboats *D. T. Lane, Eugene Dana Smith, Mary Jane* and Corps dredge *Addison* provide steam to run the pumps to raise the *Cordill* after divers built an internal bulkhead around the hole in her hull.

The *Senator Cordill* sits high and dry in early March 1927 waiting for a raise to float her free.

She sits where the Interstate Highway bridge crosses the Kanawha today, with the Fort Hill profile as a back drop.

To view this scene today, stand at the junction of Kanawha Boulevard and Tennessee Avenue.

Stern shot of the above scene taken by Captain Bill Pollock. Methods to move the *Cordill* included using a house-mover from Pittsburgh but the river did the job after about two weeks.

The *Cordill* appears to be raising steam in anticipation of floating off the Elk Chute Bar.

This scene has changed little over the last 63 years and many of the homes facing Kanawha Boulevard still remain.

During her Pittsburgh-Cincinnati days, Captain Frederick Way, Jr. was her master-pilot for three months in 1931, and her pilot in 1932, 1933 and 1934. In the early morning of February 5, 1934, before daylight, the *Cordill* was steaming up river to Pittsburgh. Captain Way was on board the *Cordill* and provides us with a vivid picture of how she would have her last sinking: "We were fighting ice and the temperature was near zero. The ice was so solid at St. Marys we couldn't get in to the wharfboat. Times were tough. Captain Hornbrook had told me that he was reducing pilot's wages to $4 a day effective at Pittsburgh. 'If you want to keep the job it's yours—if not I have a man waiting to come,' he stated. Hornbrook never equivocated in the slightest; he always stated things. If the weather had been more moderate I probably would have acceded, knowing the dire circumstances of the cash drawer. But with all that ice out there and the wind blowing I said 'Get him, whoever he is.'

The point of this is—pointed like a period—the *Cordill* never got to Pittsburgh. Early in the dark hours before daylight, Monday, February 5, 1934, she stabbed an improperly lowered wicket and down, down she went, sunk in the icy stream. Pilot Wilsie Miller was on watch but he hadn't a chance; it just happened. Herb Sidenstricker was the clerk who got me alerted and out of bed. Before I'd pulled on my shoes the lights went out. Next thing mate Wylie Hill and I were out on the starboard guard amidship on the boiler deck. He was asking, 'Do you think she'll turn over?' One glance downriver showed me where we were; just above the chamber at Lock 14 headed in for the upper guide wall—dam was down. 'No,' I was saying, 'too shallow here.' A voice in the blackness called 'I'm drowning!' Then everything was still and dark.

By instinct I took up the stairs for the roof and the pilothouse. Captain Hornbrook was out by the bell. He saw me. 'This is the end of everything,' he said quietly.

Wilsie Miller was still in the pilothouse, up there alone; there wasn't much point in leaving, for the coal stove was going and it was warm and cozy there. 'How does it feel to be on watch and have a steamboat sink under you?' I asked him. He said the whole front end raised up when the wicket stabbed the hull under the forecastle. 'I knew she was a goner right then,' he said. 'I steered her for the upper guide wall but she was sunk before we got against it; I tried to blow the distress whistle but only one toot came out and then the steam was gone. I thought oh, me!'

In the excitement one rouster had dived into the river from the tip-end of the stageplank and another had dived from the forecastle. Both were drowned. The voice Wylie Hill and I had heard was the latter. The water covered the main deck, deeper as you went aft, and I suppose there was about six feet depth in the engine room.

There was no way to get ashore although we were within twenty feet of the guide wall. The main concern was fire but a thorough check confirmed that all was well.

So everybody huddled in the forward end of the main cabin around the stove, rousters and all, and told his version of where he'd been and what he'd done. Every now and then great fields of floating ice rubbed against the outboard guard. The lock crew brought a yawl alongside just in case but nobody wanted to leave. There had been enough trouble out there in the dark.

When daylight came—a matter of four hours—the crew got the stage swung around. J. Mack Gamble drove me to Clarington where I caught a bus home. The end of the *Senator Cordill* came right there."

VIEW FROM TOP OF BANK ABOVE GUIDE WALL
SHOWING PACKET SENATOR CORDILL
LOCK & DAM N° 14. O.R.   FEB. 1934

Steamboats are a lot like people, they have their own character and eccentricities. Some are memorable, others soon forgotten.

Nobody knows steamboating better than Captain Fred Way, Jr. He was to later reflect on his time on the *Senator Cordill* and pay her this lasting tribute: "the *Cordill* was the most comfortable and satisfactory pile of lumber to pilot that I know about. In a high wind she was as deliberate as a turtle, had pretty engine room bells, and she was one of the very few boats I really anticipated coming on watch on, day or night, rain or shine."

STEAMER "SENATOR CORDILL"

Pittsburgh and Charleston

Leaves PITTSBURGH ....Tuesday, 4:00 P. M.
Leaves CHARLESTON.....Thursday, 10:00 P. M.

Last Trip of the *Liberty*

Franklin D. Roosevelt was almost through his first term and Henry Ford's little V-8 was called the fastest thing on the road. Out in California, the legendary Douglas DC-3 airliner was already on the drawing board while in Europe Adolf Hitler's fledgling army had marched into the Rhineland without opposition. The year was 1936 and on the Kanawha River, history was being made by the weary little steam packet *Liberty.*

There has to be a first and a last to everything; so it fell to the *Liberty* to bear the sad title of the last regular packet on the Great Kanawha River, thus ending over a century of passenger steamboat service to and from Charleston.

The seeds of the downfall of the river passenger packet had been sown in 1873 when the shrill whistle of the first C & O locomotive sounded out across Charleston. Sixty-three years later the combination of the railroad, Mr. Ford's automobiles and the upcoming aviation industry finally brought an end to that grand era of the steamboat travel.

The name *Liberty* has graced six other boats operating on the inland rivers, including the side-wheel excursion boat that operated in the Charleston area in 1903. However, this last packet on the Kanawha had been built in 1912 at Clarington, Ohio by the Booth family who had interest in at least three of the earlier *Libertys.*

The *Liberty's* hull was built from trees from the forest back of Clarington that were personally selected by Walter C. Booth. She was built as a "labor of love" by the Booth family without some of the newer innovations such as steam power assisted steering, however her rudder was so finely balanced that she handled with a minimum of effort by the pilot. She also had the distinction of never sinking—from the day she was launched until over 24 years later.

From 1912 until she came to the Kanawha in 1929 the *Liberty* had operated in a variety of trades on the upper Ohio River. Her arrival on the Kanawha was to work the "huckster trade" bringing chickens and eggs from the farms in the valley to the markets of Pittsburgh. Business was light at best in the beginning and did not improve with the construction of highways by Ohio and West Virginia. Motor trucks were now becoming more popular and the packet trade was fading quickly. The *Liberty* thus did her time on the Kanawha in an almost desperate race to earn a profit.

But the *Liberty* continued to operate with her open front pilot house equiped with a Burnside coal stove to scorch the pilots back side while his whiskers froze; signal bells to the engineer which were hand pulled; a carbon-arc searchlight that was raised, lowered and turned by baling wire and sash cord; speaking tubes to carry commands from the pilot to the office and engineers and a large "lazy bench" elevated in the rear. In short, the *Liberty* was an anachronism—hung up on the shoals of time, circa 1890. Probably that simplicity was one reason she paddled her way into 1936 when bigger and grander boats had long gone to the wreckers. Captain Walter Booth once estimated that the venerable little steamboat had covered 550,000 miles in her 24 years.

In 1930 prohibition was in full effect and all manner of schemes were devised to transport bootleg whiskey. So it was that the *Liberty* was seized at Charleston by Federal agents. They charged that several of her officers and crew had on more than one occasion brought illegal whiskey to Charleston from Pittsburgh. Others accused of this crime included a "huckster" from St. Marys, West Virginia and the Charleston wharfboat proprietor.

Allegedly the whiskey had been sent on barrels labeled "chinaware" to a capital city street address. About a week before Christmas the case went to the jury and luckily for the *Liberty* "gang", they were found not guilty because the jury felt that the Federal agents had gone to great effort to "set up" the rivermen.

The *Liberty* continued to run in the Pittsburgh-Charleston trade outlasting her competitors. But times were changing and business continued to decline. In early June 1936 word finally came down from the Pittsburgh office to "throw in the towel." The *Liberty* had been contracted to tow a showboat, so on a bright summer day the last regular packet operating on the upper Ohio River pulled away from the Charleston wharf. There was no big crowd to bid the boat farewell because the local papers had made little note of this historic event. It was felt by some that another packet would take her place when the business picked up, but not many, for the newer modes of transportation were doing what the packetboats had always done before—and after all the big steam tow boats were still running up and down the river.

Liberty's Cabin, 1934.
Captain C. W. Stoll Photo.

Steamer *Liberty* at Charleston, W. Va., September 1, 1934. Moored below the wharfboat which is sunk. Pictured is left to right: Clark Query, Captain Walter Booth and purser Roy Collett. Captain C. W. Stoll Photo.

The *Liberty* began towing the showboat *Golden-rod* which was carrying the well known "Major Bowles Amateur Hour." During this period, Major Bowles show was broadcast nationwide on radio and was one of the most popular shows of its day.

The showboat towing job only lasted one season and the *Liberty* found herself in Cairo, Illinois and after weathering the flood of 1936 was without a future.

She was bought and brought back to Parkersburg for repairs. On July 27, 1938, Captain Ben Rike bought her for $195.00 and towed her to Kanauga, Ohio across the river from Pt. Pleasant—and there she was dismantled. As was the case of so many of the old steamboats, her engines were saved and placed on the steamer *Valley Belle*, another Kanawha River packet that had been converted into a towboat.

Steamer *Liberty's* engines being transferred to Steamer *Valley Belle* at Captain Ralph Raike's landing at Kanauga, Ohio in 1939. Captain C. W. Stoll Photo.

The Tradition Continues

The Great Kanawha River continues to produce steamboatmen of exceptional skills and abilities.

The following is Captain Clarke C. Hawley's own account of how he became a steamboat pilot and master for the steamer *Natchez* of New Orleans.

The Kanawha River was a mighty stream when, as a little boy, I first remember seeing it at flood stage in the 1930's. I'll never forget the sight of all sorts of drift, trees, outhouses, etc., gliding under Charleston's Southside Bridge. My next recollection was of *Bryant's Showboat* at the Charleston city front with calliope blaring. My father obligingly parked his car on the newly constructed Kanawha Boulevard so I could get a better view of the whistles and their fascinating steam music.

In the late 1940's I saw the *Gordon G. Greene* at the State Capitol steps during one of her weekly forays up from Cincinnati. The *Avalon* called on Charleston once or twice a year in the early 1950's and I still remember the sound of that wonderful whistle echo bouncing off the South Hills across the river.

I was a copyboy and wire-photo operator at the *Charleston Daily Mail* at the time Brother Ken's Junior High School took an afternoon "matinee" trip on the *Avalon*, and I went along as his guest. The smell of steam, cylinder oil, and popcorn was a heady combination that met one upon boarding. Newly loaded "black diamond" dust crunched underfoot and steam spewed out the "possumbelly" drains at waterlevel making gurgling sounds with each slight wave. Sounds and smells never forgotten and still enjoyed.

Only one thing was missing... the calliope... strangely silent but expected. About halfway downstream to Blaines Island I mistakenly assumed that a distinguished-looking Watchman was the Captain and asked him about the calliope. Seems that the regular player had quit a week earlier and the piano player in the band couldn't handle the mechanical action. I was led up to the pilot house where a skeptical Captain Ernest Wagner asked what led me to believe I could play a calliope. When I responded that I could play without music and had a parlor organ at home, he agreed to let me try it, with the provision that I turn it off at once if he signaled. He rang for steam by tapping the gong and led me back on the roof to that strange musical contraption that was, by this time, banging and nearly errupting with just-admitted steam. I was too short to reach the key-board so the captain extracted a wooden Coca-Cola case from beneath the pilot house and I stepped up to a new career.

After I thumped out a couple of tunes, Captain stopped me to ask if I had a summer job and would I like to be a full-time calliope player. Always the straight-shooter, he agreed that he couldn't match my $35.00 weekly journalistic salary, but could pay $27.50 with room and board. He could equal the $35.00 only if I popped corn as a side line. He agreed that I "would not get rich but would see lots of scenery"... then reeled off the summer itinerary which took the *Avalon* up to Montgomery, on around to Pittsburgh, then to Nashville, St. Paul, Stillwater, Joliet, Memphis, etc.

All that river geography peaked my interest, but what about the *Daily Mail*? My mentor at the paper was a talented reporter/historian, Adrian Gwin, who advised me to "get on that boat" explaining that I "could work for a newspaper anytime and that the tramping routine of the *Avalon* would be an education in life and travel."

My father was more cautious and a little skepti-cal of the carnival atmosphere of excursion boats and did not share my mother's enthusiasm which was as keen as that of my reporter/mentor.

Mother's family, the Calverts, had worked the upper Kanawha for years and had owned the ill-fated *Kanawha Belle, Mockingbird, J. Q. Dickenson* and others, and her father, M. G. Campbell, had been a steamboat "clerk." If river work had been good for them it would be good for me. Enough said!

Captain Wagner assured my good parents that he would look after me as if I was his, moved me into his quarters, and my river career was launched at the foot of Summers Street.

I worked the faithful *Avalon* until her tramping days were over in the Fall of 1961, and served as calliope player, popcorn-popper, deckhand, watchman, mate and master. In 1959 I took a sabbatical leave, with Captain Wagner's blessing and joined the *Delta Queen* as mate. This move enabled me to log higher tonnage and earn an all-gross-ton Masters license in 1959 and to rejoin the *Avalon* as mate and alternate master for her 1960-1961 seasons.

In 1962 the *Avalon* laid-up in a cloud of dwin-dling business and bankruptcy. The popularity of television and advent of cheap air conditioning in middle America had changed public tastes and no longer was a boat ride the best way to cool off and be entertained. Captain Wagner and I joined the *Delta Queen* in 1962 as master and alternate mas-ter. Soon after our *Avalon* advance agent Betty Blake came aboard as Mrs. Greene's secretary. In 1966-67 I served as Mrs. Greene's Vice President and General Manager.

In 1970 I resigned the *Delta Queen* to once again join, as master, my old friend, the refur-bished *Avalon* now proudly operating as the *Belle of Louisville*. Even though I haven't worked the *Belle* for over 15 years, some of my most cher-ished memories are with her as I learned the trade on her decks and experienced those hard and demanding years in the "tramping trade" on eight rivers and through 17 states. From Summers Street I ended up on the beautiful *Natchez*, a modern-day version of the *Virginia*.

Steamer NATCHEZ

Sternwheeler COTTON BLOSSOM

Riverboat BAYOU JEAN LAFITTE

NEW ORLEANS STEAMBOAT COMPANY

Towboat River

Steamer *Ella Layman* and small unknown towboat with a fleet of Crown Hill coal mine wood barges. The Ella Layman Towboat Co. of Charleston was named for this boat and was owned by Colonel Bob Carr. Prior to coming to the Kanawha River, the *Layman* had towed oil products for Standard Oil Co. from Pittsburgh to Huntington and other upper Ohio River locations from 1872 to the early 1880s.

As early as 1829, Kanawha River steamboats were towing keelboats to Maysville, Kentucky and Cincinnati. The keelboats were secured to the sides of the steamboats, not pushed ahead of the boat as is done today, however the following year the first towboat appeared on the river. She was the *Enterprise* under the command of Captain James A. Payne.

It was during this period that the Kanawha was one of the most important natural tributaries of the Ohio River. With its' source of vast natural resources including salt, coal and timber, the development of boats to handle these items developed quickly.

The shipment of coal on the Kanawha began when Alva Hansford filled a flatboat full of coal in 1840 and sent it to Cincinnati. From this there grew the coal mining/river shipment industry that exists today. The growth of this industry is reflected by the fact that over 46 coal companies were started in the Kanawha valley between 1847 and 1860.

A Charleston newspaper reported the following steamboats were operating on the Kanawha and Elk Rivers in early May 1876; *Lookout* (t), *Daniel Boone* (p), *West Virginia* (p), *Modoc* (t/p), *Judge Baker* (t), *Ianthe* (t), *D. T. Lane* (t), *Oil Valley* (t), *H. E. Pierpoint* (t), *Hawkeye* (t), *Phil*

*(t) towboat   (p) packet

Morgan (p), *John W. Morgan* (t), *Peytona* (t), *Stella* (t), *Ed Smith* (p), *Julia No. 2* (p), *Tom Farrow* (t), *Alex Chambers* (t), *Lizzie Gardner* (t), *Mount Clare* (t), and *Elk River Surprise* (t), which navigated the Elk River 90 miles.

As can be seen from this early listing, most of the boats were towboats indicating that there was a great demand for their services.

In 1880 Mr. George W. Patton wrote a report for the Corps of Engineers concerning the placement of a railroad bridge across the Kanawha River for the Elk Railroad to unite with the Chesapeake and Ohio Railroad. In deciding the height of the bridge and the distance between the piers, Mr. Patton chose two packets and two towboats to determine an acceptable distance.

The packets *Boone* and *Telephone* and the towboats *D. T. Lane* and *Liberty* were listed as the largest boats operating on the Kanawha. Since Mr. Patton was using the height of the pilothouses and chimneys (smokestacks) above the water, the following figures were used for the height: *Boone*—37.2, 49.1; *Telephone*—36.0, 46.9; *D. T. Lane*—33.2, 50.7; and *Liberty*—34.8, 52.6. It was also observed that the average number of barges in a tow ranged from 11 to 13.

Based on these findings, it was recommended that, if built, the bridge should have a channel span of not less than 250 feet and an overhead clear space of not less than 70 feet by the reading on the Charleston gauge.

The legacy of the steam towboats can be seen today on the Kanawha River with the passing of the diesel towboat and their barges. The cheapest ton/mile shipment in America.

*(t) towboat   (p) packet

Looking down stream near the "lower ferry" at Charleston with the towboats *Little Samson* and *Iron Cliff* and a fleet of loaded coal barges. The coal barges were generally 25 feet wide, 130 feet long with a draft of 6 to 7 feet. Each barge would, on average, be loaded with 6½ feet; 14,000 bushels or 560 tons.

The *Little Samson* was built at Cincinnati in 1880 for Captain David Stout and towed coal from the Kanawha River to Cincinnati with the *Iron Cliff*. The *Iron Cliff* was acquired by Captain Stout from its Pittsburgh owners after a short period of service on the upper Ohio. Built in 1881, the *Iron Cliff* was sold to Greenville, Mississippi in 1896.

Ice condition on the Kanawha River at the mouth of the Elk River, January, 1879.

All three of the boats pictured survived this potential disaster. The packet *Telephone* continued to operate on the Kanawha until 1885. The towboat *Liberty No. 4* built in 1863, did sink from ice damage but was raised and continued to operate by the Campbell's Creek Coal Co. The towboat *Lookout* was built in 1870 and towed Kanawha River salt to Nashville, Tennessee until dismantled in 1880.

Statement of coal shipped from Great Kanawha mines, below Kanawha Falls, during years ending June 30, 1881, June 1, 1883, and June 1, 1884.

Names of operators.	Year ending June 30, 1881.			Year ending June 1, 1883.			Year ending June 1, 1884.		
	By rail.	By river.	Total.	By rail.	By river.	Total.	By rail.	By river.	Total.
Bennington Colliery	....	530,684	530,684	....	394,000	394,000	(*)	(*)	(*)
Black Band Iron and Coal Company	....						102,240	309,848	412,0..
Buck, Stuart M.*									
Campbell's Creek Coal Company	....	2,409,260	2,409,260	....	3,070,463	3,070,463	....	4,131,711	4,131,..
Cannelton Coal Company	840,000	....	840,000	1,068,045	....	1,068,045	(*)	(*)	(*)
Carver Bros	783,188	266,000	1,049,188	1,313,340	....	1,313,340	980,000	....	980,0..
Cedar Grove Mining Company				....	520,000	520,000	....	183,000	183,0..
Coal Valley Coal Company	948,192	....	948,192	1,015,960	....	1,015,960	698,861	....	698,8..
Crescent Mines				2,016,000	....	2,016,000	1,746,102	....	1,746,..
Crowen Hill Splint Coal Company				610,260	272,604	882,864	401,932	650,000	1,051,..
Dana Bros	....	760,144	760,144	....	1,899,789	1,899,789	....	1,751,439	1,751,..
Davis, M. T., & Co.				1,102,892	....	1,102,892	977,840	....	977,8..
Eagle Coal and Coke Works				1,497,810	....	1,497,810	1,569,700	....	1,569,..
Faulkner, F.				775,202	8,355	783,557	785,344	5,040	790,3..
Great Kanawha Colliery Company							180,878	....	180,8..
Henson & Talley				269,629	....	269,629			
Kanawha Cannel Coal Company				50,000	608,000	658,000	145,544	346,600	492,..
Kanawha Mining Company				613,933	337,296	951,229	650,137	1,279,256	1,929,..
Logan Coal and Salt Company				†400,000	....	400,000			
Macfarlane Coal Company							714,000	....	714,..
Mannet Mining Company	....	2,409,260	2,409,260	....	1,601,188	1,601,188	....	1,853,416	1,853,..
Mount Morris Coal Company	481,320	23,800	505,120	700,000	....	700,000	773,612	....	773,6..
Oak Ridge Coal Company									
Peabody Coal Company	....	311,024	311,024	....	1,012,234	1,012,234	....	1,500,000	1,500,0..
Pioneer Coal Company		*2,409,260	2,409,260	....	1,848,715	1,848,715	....	1,730,864	1,730,8..
Reynolds & Sturdevant							35,280	8,316	43,..
Robinson Coal Company	1,643,824	70,112	1,713,936	631,107	917,300	1,548,407	865,592	909,501	1,775,0..
Saint Clair Company				190,000	....	190,000	448,200	....	448,..
Stevens Coal and Coke Company							28,000		28,0..
Straughan, George (Coal Valley)	918,316	90,356	1,008,672	762,227	....	762,227	139,724	....	139,..
Straughan, George (North Coaling)				....	980,000	980,000			
Winifrede Coal Company				199,868	1,325,791	1,525,659	226,426	2,337,190	2,563,6..
Wyoming Manufacturing Company				242,564	....	242,564			
Other parties	1,016,820	348,796	1,365,616	261,418	174,723	436,141	1,303,760	711,903	2,015,6..
Total, bushels	6,631,660	9,628,696	16,260,356	13,290,255	15,370,458	28,660,713	12,059,172	18,421,084	30,480,2..

* Included below in other parties.   † Estimated.

A. M. SCOTT,
Assistant Engineer.

Sections of a report prepared by the Corps of Engineers listing the number of mines operating on the Kanawha and the bushels shipped during the early 1880s.

Coal shipped from mines on the Great Kanawha River below Kanawha Falls, and other statistics relating to the coal business for the several years named.

Year.	Shipments by river.	Shipments by railroad.	Total shipment.	Mines in operation.	Towboats in use.	Coal-barges in use.
	Bushels.	Bushels.	Bushels.	No.	No.	No.
1875	4,048,300	*5,792,925	9,841,225	8	5	†150
1876	5,024,050	*6,609,650	11,633,700	10	5	....
1877	5,183,650	*7,758,800	12,942,450	10	5	....
Year ending June 30, 1881	9,628,696	6,631,660	16,260,356	13	6	....
Year ending June 1, 1883	15,370,458	13,290,255	28,660,713	26	14	430
Year ending June 1, 1884	18,421,084	12,059,172	30,480,256	28	14	....
Year ending June 1, 1885	17,812,323	12,972,217	30,784,540	32	22	....
Year ending June 1, 1886	17,861,613	13,953,745	31,815,358	36	24	854
Year ending June 1, 1887	23,233,374	19,160,896	42,394,270	37	....	....

Compare the number of mines operating on the Kanawha River with the number of towboats running on the river. The building of the locks and dams had a major impact on these figures.

* The shipments by railroad for the first three years given, viz, 1875, 1876, 1877, include the New River mines above Kanawha Falls.
†About.

Respectfully submitted.

A. M. SCOTT,
Assistant Engineer.

Col. WM. P. CRAIGHILL,
Corps of Engineers U. S. A.

— 134 —

Early photograph of the steamer *Mount Clare* on the
Kanawha, circa 1870. Probably at or near Buffalo and
taken by Dr. Claudius Pitrat (See Chapter II).

Built in 1868 at Wheeling to tow barges for the B & O Railroad
Wheeling. Named for their shops at Mount Clare, Maryland, the
Mount Clare was bought by the Marmet Coal Company to tow coal
out of the Kanawha River. She was dismantled in 1903 with her
engines going to the *Lucie Marmet*.

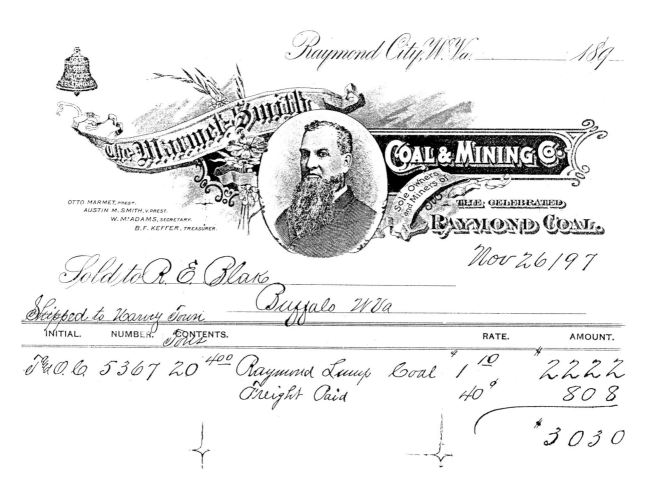

Raymond City, W. Va. _____ 189_

The Marmet-Smith Coal & Mining Co.

OTTO MARMET, PREST.
AUSTIN M. SMITH, V.PREST.
W. MᶜADAMS, SECRETARY.
B.F. KEFFER, TREASURER.

Sole Owners and Miners of THE CELEBRATED RAYMOND COAL.

Nov 26/97

Sold to R. E. Black   Buffalo W Va

Shipped to Harvy Town

INITIAL.	NUMBER.	CONTENTS. Tons		RATE.	AMOUNT.
M O C	5367	20 ⁴⁰⁰	Raymond Lump Coal	$1 ¹⁰	$2222
			Freight Paid	40 ¢	808
					$3030

The *Otto Marmet* like all of the Marmet boat was noted for the large amount of yellow paint used on it; stern bulkhead, door shutters, etc. She was built in 1898 at Raymond City, W. Va. and towed Kanawha River coal to Cincinnati. Burned at North Bend, Ohio company landing in 1935.

Named for Mr. Florence Marmet, brother of Otto Marmet when built in 1900, the *Florence Marmet* towed coal between the Kanawha River and Cincinnati for the Otto Marmet Coal & Mining Co. She carried a large gilded eagle on top of her pilothouse that had been made for a G.A.R. float for a parade at Cincinnati. Condemned in 1915 and not rebuilt.

Rebuilt from the *Mount Clare* in 1903, the *Lucie Marmet* towed coal between the Kanawha River and Cincinnati. On October 5, 1914, while moored at Charleston, the *Lucie Marmet* caught fire and burned to the water's edge.

Built at Marietta, Ohio in 1911 and owned by the Otto Marmet Coal & Mining Co., the *Sallie Marmet* was used to tow Kanawha River coal to Cincinnati. She sank above Lock and Dam No. 36, Ohio River in 1925. When divers went down to raise her they found her hull punctured by a huge, old-time anchor. It was thought to have been from one of the ocean going brigs built in the Marietta area prior to 1850. The anchor is now on display at Tu-Endi-We Park, Pt. Pleasant. The *Sallie Marmet* was dismantled in 1935.

Steamer Sallie Marmet, Interior - Engine Room.

Built at Pittsburgh in 1878 and owned by the Marmet Coal Co., the *George Matheson* towed out of Pittsburgh early in her career. She was moved to the Kanawha later. Sank in the ice at Cincinnati in January 1893. The wreck was sold and the new owner raised the *Matheson* and operated her until 1906.

The "Bologna George" as she was known on the river was built in 1907 to tow coal for the Hatfield coal and river interest. The *George Matheson No. 2* was renamed *W. C. Mitchell* in October 1920 by the Hatfield-Campbell Coal Co. and continued to tow coal between the Kanawha River and Cincinnati until retired in 1939.

Looking almost as busy as Cincinnati, this winter scene is misleading. The Charleston waterfront was never this crowded under normal circumstances. These sternwheelers are taking shelter from the ice floes which could easily damage their wooden hulls. This photo clearly shows the central steeple of the Kanawha County Courthouse complete with the statue of Justice at its peak. Further east, up the river, the faint outline of the pointed spires of both the old Kanawha Valley Bank and the Ruffner Hotel are seen.

ICE-BOUND.

A List of River Boats Tied Up Along Kanawha River Here and Below.

The following boats are ice-bound the Kanawha river at Point Pleasant: Convoy, Hawk, Ida Budd, Bob Prichard, D. T. Lane, Jennie Campbell, Annie L., Ocean Wave, Dick Brown, Vesper, Homer B., and a tow of steel rails belonging to the Gray Iron Line of Pittsburg, Pa. In and around Charleston: Mt. Claire, at Raymond City; Ben Wood, Spring Hill, Lydia, Handy No. 2, T. D. Dale, Coal Bluff, Bee, Mascot, Government dredge boat, Alex Montgomery, Alex Martin, Wm. Ernst, Iron Cliff, Winifrede, and G. T. Thayer.

The second of three towboats named *Winifrede* that worked on the Kanawha enters the lock at Lock and Dam No. 6, September 26, 1892. Built at Charleston, W. Va. by the Winifrede Coal Co. in 1890, this *Winifrede* burned in 1897.

The Corps of Engineers towboat *Bee* (note "B" on pilothouse) locking through recently completed Lock No. 6. Built at Charleston, W. Va. in 1881, the *Bee* was used in the construction of the first series of locks and dams on the Kanawha.

Locks and Dams

ON THE GREAT KANAWHA RIVER.

What the Government Has Done to Improve Navigation.

The United States Government has appropriated three million eight hundred and eighty-five thousand and two hundred dollars, ($3,885,200) for creating slack water navigation on the Great Kanawha river from the Ohio river at Pt. Pleasant to a point near the Kanawha Falls, in Fayette county, W. Va., distance ninety miles.

With this money the following locks and dams have been constructed towit:

Lock and Dam No 2, near Cannelton. Finished in 1887.

Lock and Dam No. 3, near Paint Creek. Finished in 1882.

Lock and Dam No. 4, near Coalburg. Finished in 1880.

Lock and Dam No. 5, near Brownstown. Finished in 1880.

Lock and Dam No. 6, below Charleston. Finished in 1886.

Lock and Dam No. 7, below St. Albans. Finished in 1893.

Lock and Dam No. 8, below Raymond City. Finished in 1893.

Locks and Dams Nos. 9, 10 and 11, now under construction, and nearly finished, are located as follows:

Lock and Dam No. 9, above Buffalo.

Lock and Dam No. 10, below Buffalo.

Lock and Dam No. 11, near Pt. Pleasant, at the mouth of the river.

This entire slack water navigation will be completed for the 90 miles when Locks and Dams Nos. 9, 10 and 11 are finished, which will be in the year 1897.

This important government work is now in charge of Col. Peter C. Hains, of Baltimore. The U. S. Resident Engineer is Addison M. Scott, whose office is in this city.

COAL SHIPMENTS.

The shipment of coal in bushels from the colleries on the Great Kanawha river, below the Kanawha Falls, for fiscal years (ending June 30th) by river, and for several years by railroad, is given in the following table, which has been furnished us by the Resident Engineer:

Year.	River.	Rail.	Total.
1875	4,048,300	———	———
1876	5,024,000	———	———
1877	5,183,600	———	———
1878	no report	———	———
1879	" "	———	———
18-0	" "	———	———
1881	9 628,696	6,631,660	16,260,356
1882	no report	———	———
1883	15,370,418	13,290,255	28,660,713
1884	18,421 084	12,059,172	30,480,256
1885	17 812,323	12,972,217	30,784,540
1886	17 861,613	13,953 745	31,815,358
1887	23,233,374	19,160,896	42,394,270
1888	20,100,525	20,962,686	41,063,611
1889	26,921,788	22,031,121	48,842,909
1890	24,161,554	27,433,925	51,591,979
1891	25,761,316	28,608,025	54,429,371
1892	26,787,888	30 844,100	57,631,888
1893	22,983,000	no report	———
1894	25,821,000	" "	———
1895	21,882,600	" "	———
1896	23,050,000	" "	———

The first two locks and dams of the system, as noted above, were completed in 1880.

If such has been the increase of the coal traffic from the locks and dams already constructed and in operation, how much greater will that increase be when locks and dams No. 9, 10 and 11 are completed, and thereby six feet of water for 90 miles on the Great Kanawha will be furnished during the entire year?

We will here add that the shipments during the last four years have been materially cut down by unusually low water in the Great Kanawha below the locks and dams already constructed—that is, below lock and dam No. 8, situated below Raymond City. This will, however, no longer be the case after locks and dams 9, 10 and 11, now under contract, are completed. It may be added that the coal shipments by river particularly during the last two years, have also been materially affected by the prevailing "hard times"—the depression in manufacturing, and in business generally.

FREE NAVIGATION.

By an act of Congress passed in 1882, the navigation of the Great Kanawha was made free and no tolls are charged thereon.

On the Monongahela river tolls are charged thereon by the Monongahela Navigation Company which was chartered by the Legislature of Pennsylvania many years ago, with authority to lock and dam the Monongahela river and charge tolls thereon. The Kanawha river being free of tolls gives the Kanawha coal operators a very great advantage over the Monongahela coal operators.

Furthermore this free slackwater navigation is a permanent guarantee that the coal operators on the Great Kanawha river and its tributaries, Elk and Coal rivers, cannot be controlled in their shipment of coal westward by freight rates of either Chesapeake & Ohio R. R., or the Kanawha & Michigan R. R. which roads are constructed on and along the banks of the Great Kanawha river. This slackwater navigation will always furnish the Kanawha collieries with free transportation to Point Pleasant on the Ohio River.

ADVANTAGES ON THE OHIO.

Pittsburg is 262 miles by the Ohio river above Point Pleasant, and the coal boating stages are therefore more frequent at Point Pleasant than at Pittsburg.

From gauge records kept at Pittsburg and Point Pleasant for a number of years, as shown by U. S. Engineer reports, it appears there are, on an average, 155 days in a year when coal boats and barges drawing six feet of water can be taken down the Ohio from Pittsburg, whilst there are, on an average, 251 days in the year when coal boats and barges drawing the same depth of water can be taken down the Ohio river from Point Pleasant at the mouth of the Great Kanawha river.

FREEDOM FROM ICE.

The Great Kanawha, owing mainly no doubt to its source being so far south (New river, the principal tributary, rises in North Carolina), is but little obstructed by ice. Records kept at the U. S. Engineers office here show that during the last twenty-three years (beginning with 1873) navigation on the Great Kanawha has been suspended wholly or in part, an aggregate of only 195 days, or on an average less than 8½ days per year. The longest suspension was 30 days in the winter of 1892-3. During eight of the twenty three winters there was no suspension on the Great Kanawha by ice.

COMMERCIAL ADVANTAGES.

The great commercial advantages yet to be given to the coal and timber lands of the Great Kanawha and its tributaries, Elk river, Coal river, &c., will be seen when locks and dams 9, 10 and 11 are completed. That is, when ninety miles of slackwater navigation of the Great Kanawha are completed, collieries on the Great Kanawha, Elk & Coal rivers will have very great advantages over those on the Monongahela and Youghiogheny rivers in the shipments of coal down the Ohio to the western and southwestern markets.—*From Kanawha Gazette, West Va., April 21, 1897.*

Great Kanawha Coal Shipments.

Extract from the Annual Report of Chief of Engineers U. S. A., for 1889.

U. S. ENGINEER OFFICE,
CHARLESTON-KANAWHA, W. VA.,
July 30th, 1889.

Statement showing the number of bushels of Coal shipped from the Great Kanawha Valley, *below Kanawha Falls*, for the several years named:

Year of 12 Months Ending	Shipments by River.	Shipments by Railroad.	Total Shipments.	No. Mines Operated.
June 30, 1881.	9,628,696	6,631,660	16,260,356	13
June 1, 1883.	15,370,458	13,290,255	28,660,713	26
" " 1884.	18,421,084	12,059,172	30,480,256	28
" " 1885	17,812,323	12,972,217	30,784,540	32
" " 1886.	17,861,613	13,953,745	31,815,358	36
" " 1887.	23,233,374	19,160,896	42,394,270	37
" " 1888.	20,100,625	20,962,686	41,063,311	36
" " 1889.	26,921,788	22,031,121	48,952,909	36

The statement for the last year was, as usual, made up from detailed reports to this office, from all of the mines. It will be noticed that the output for the last year was considerably (nearly 16 per cent.) greater than ever before; the increase by river alone, over the former maximum (1887) being over three and a half millions of bushels.

Respectfully submitted,
ADDISON M. SCOTT,
Resident Engineer.

TO COL. WM. P. CRAIGHILL,
Corps of Engineers.

TABLE

Showing the Location, &c., of Locks and Dams on the Great Kanawha River, already Completed, now Building, and yet to be Built:

No. of Lock and Dam.	LOCATION.	Kind of Dam.	
No. 2	1 mile below Cannelton and 84¼ miles from mouth of river.	Fixed.	Finished in 1887.
" 3	1 " " Paint Creek " 79¼ " " " " "	"	" " 1882.
" 4	1½ " " Coalburg " 73 " " " " "	Movable.	" " 1880.
" 5	9 " above CHARLESTON " 67¼ " " " " "	"	" " 1880.
" 6	4½ " below " " 54 " " " " "	"	" " 1886.
" 7	1¼ " " St. Albans " 44 " " " " "	"	Now Building.
" 8	2½ " " Raymond City " 35¾ " " " " "	"	" "
" 9	6 " " Winfield " 26 " " " " "	"	Not begun yet.
" 10	2¾ " " Buffalo " 18½ " " " " "	"	" " "
" 11	Foot Three Mile Bar " 1¾ " " " " "	"	" " "

U. S. ENGINEER OFFICE,
CHARLESTON-KANAWHA, W. VA.,
JANUARY, 1890.

The impact of the completion of the first lock and dam system on the Kanawha River is illustrated by these leaflets printed in the late 1880s. With the completion of the ten lock and dams (No. 1 was never built), the Kanawha became the nation's first river to have a complete navigation system.

Our Coal Business.

OVER 42 MILLION BUSHELS SHIPPED FROM THE GREAT KANAWHA MINES BELOW KANAWHA FALLS DURING THE LAST YEAR, BIG INCREASE OVER FORMER YEARS.

[From the Kanawha Gazette.]

A statistical report recently made at the U. S Engineer office in this city, of the amount of Coal shipped from mines on the Great Kanawha during the past year is a very gratifying one, showing a decided increase in the business both by river and by railroad. The statement was compiled to accompany the annual report of Mr. A. M. Scott, Resident Engineer of the Great Kanawha Improvement, to Col. Wm. P. Craighill, the officer in charge. It was derived (like the Great Kanawha coal statements for several years past, published in the annual reports of the Chief of Engineers), from statistics furnished to the U. S. Engineer office from every coal mine in the Valley and is regarded as accurate. It shows the total amount shipped from the Valley, below the Falls, during the year ending June, 1887, was 42,394,270 bushels. Of this 23,233,347 bushels went out by river and 19,160,896 by rail.

The report for the year before, being to June, 1886, was the largest up to that time, showed the total shipment for that year to be 31,815,358 bushels; of which 17,861,613 was by river and 13,953,745 by rail.

It appears that during the past year the output of coal on the Great Kanawha has increased fully 33 per cent. over any previous year. Over 10½ millions bushels more coal was shipped than in any year before.

It will be noticed, too, that this increase is about equally divided between the shipments by river and by railroad.

The *Annie L.* towed cross ties, brick and coal
during her career from 1881 to 1907. Built at
Murraysville, W. Va., she burned at Mt.
Vernon, Indiana.

Steamer *Convoy* waits at the mouth of the Kanawha
River for a rise to start for Cincinnati with another
coal tow. Built in 1888, the *Convoy* towed coal from
the upper Ohio or Kanawha until she capsized in a
windstorm at Cincinnati in 1915.

Photo courtesy of Daniel E. Davidson

Railroad transfer operations on the Kanawha before the railroad bridge was built. The steam train engine is preparing to pull the box cars off the ferry flat being held in position by towboat on the north side of the river near the present capitol, circa 1909.

The *Scout* positioning the transfer flats on the south side of the river. She was teamed with the *Bob Ballard* at both Charleston and in the Ashland-Ironton area towing railroad transfer barges.

The *Scout* began her career in 1903 towing transfer barges for the Kanawha & Ohio Transfer Co. For the most of her career, she was used in the construction of the locks and dams on the Ohio River.

Built as a packet in 1890, the *Bob Ballard* ran in the Gallipolis-Marietta trade. Unique feature of the *Ballard* was that she had a tin roof.

Rebuilt as a towboat, she was used to tow transfer barges. Sank in 1909.

The *John Dana* was built in 1888 and was owned by the Campbell's Creek Coal Co. She towed between Kanawha River and Cincinnati and below. Her 1892 crew; Captain E. A. Burnside, master; Harry Burnside and Charels E. Morris, pilots. Lew Lear and William D. Curry, cub pilots got in yawls at Point Pleasant in October, in dead low water, and rowed to Cincinnati. They arrived in time to see the *Columbus* river celebration as guests on the *George Matheson*. She burned in Dana, W. Va. in 1893.

Steamer *W. B. Calderwood* passing Ironton, Ohio. Named for the superintendant of mines at Dana, W. Va. when purchased by the Campbell's Creek Coal Company in 1895. The *Calderwood* towed coal between the Kanawha River and Cincinnati until 1912 when she was dismantled. Her boilers were then transferred to the new Kanawha River towboat *Eugene Dana Smith*.

For 66 years there was a *D. T. Lane* on the Kanawha River. The first *D. T. Lane* (above) was built at Pittsburgh in 1871 by David T. Lane using engines from the packet *Ingomar* that had been built out of the Civil War gunboat *General Thomas*.

Acquired about 1875 by S. F. Dana and James H. Santz to tow coal out of the Kanawha River. Became a part of the Campbell's Creek Coal Co. in 1880. Dismantled in 1908 at Dana, W. Va. to build the second *D. T. Lane* (below).

The "Rowdy Dick from Campbell's Creek" as she was known by Kanawha rivermen. Built from the first *D. T. Lane* in 1908 at Dana, W. Va., the *Lane* became a Kanawha River institution with everybody at Campbell's Creek working on the *Lane* at one time or another. She was retired at Dana, W. Va. and sank there in June 1934 and was finally dismantled in October 1937.

Point Pleasant, W. Va.,
August 18, 1908.

You are cordially invited to be present at the launching

of our new Steamer

D. T. Lane,

Dana-on-Kanawha, W. Va., 10 A. M.

Saturday, August 22, 1908.

E. A. Burnside,

Manager of Transportation.

On March 25, 1917, the *Plymouth* sank below Lock and Dam No. 3, Kanawha River. The cook was drowned. This was not this boat's first accident for the *R. L. Aubrey*, as she was named when built in 1899. The *Aubrey* sank at Louisville on July 7, 1906 and her boilers exploded on March 14, 1910. She was raised, rebuilt and renamed *Plymouth* by the E. J. Hicky Transportation Co. for their town and mines at Plymouth, W. Va., Kanawha River.

STR. PLYMOUTH, TURNED OVER MAR 17, 1917 AT LOCK 3 ON KANAWHA RIVER

The *Plymouth* on the marine ways at Paducah, Kentucky in 1926. Note the shallow flat bottomed hull, a feature of all Western Rivers steamboats since 1816 when Henry Shreve built the packet *Washington* at Wheeling, Virginia.

After the Lock No. 3 sinking, the *Plymouth* was repaired and continued to tow coal to Cincinnati. Acquired by the American Barge Line and rebuilt at Paducah in 1926, the *Plymouth* was retired at Jeffersonville, Indiana and sank there on January 14, 1945.

The *E. R. Andrews*, with its hull with steel sides and frame and heavy oak bottom, was the first boat of steel construction on the Kanawha River. She was the pride-and-joy of the Campbell's Creek Coal Company and especially its manager of transportation, Captain E.A. Burnside. Built in 1894, the *Andrews* was a boat of many innovations; from its steel/wood hull to its wireless telegraph, possibly the first on the inland rivers.

She towed coal from the Kanawha River to Cincinnati and Louisville for 16 years. Bought by the Barrett Line in 1912 who changed her name to *Oscar E. Barrett*.

Two of the Kanawha River's finest towboats showing the difference in the type of towboat construction. The *E. R. Andrews* with its pilot-house setting on her roof amidship was of traditional construction while the *Robert P. Gillham* with its pilot-house set on the boiler (second) deck forward of the cabin was referred as a pool-style towboat.

E. R. Andrews at Buffalo, W. Va. with an excursion for the benefit of the Ladies Missionary Society of the Point Pleasant Presbyterian Church, June 29, 1899. The trip was from Pt. Pleasant to Armour's Creek and return.

The relationship between the boat captains and owners and the communities in which the boats docked often lead to the towboats being used for social or church function such as this.

CAPT. E. A. BURNSIDE DROWNS

TOWBOAT HELPER
TURNS TURTLE
AT CINCINNATI

Designed and built under the supervision of Captain E. A. Burnside for the Campbell's Creek Coal Co. in 1920. The *Helper* (2nd) was built using parts from *Helper* (1st) that had been built in 1917.

On March 16, 1922, Captain Burnside was piloting the *Helper* in the Cincinnati harbor during high water with one of the outboard rudders removed contributing to the *Helper* turning over, drowning the captain.

On board at the time was A. J. Schletker and his wife. Mrs. Schletker also lost her life in the accident. The *Helper* was raised, rebuilt and renamed *Ed Moore*.

The measure of E.A. Burnsides reputation can best be illustrated by the story of the Monongahela River deckhand, while on vacation, who took the train to Point Pleasant. Upon leaving the train, the deckhand hailed a cab and told the driver, "There's three things us guys up in the pools are always hearing about; Captain E. A. Burnside, the *Robert P. Gillham* and Red House Chute—take me to 'em."

Named for Col. Robert P. Gillham who started in the coal business at the age of 15 with G.W.C. Johnson. Later others joined these men and they in turn became a part of the Campbell's Creek Coal Co. The *Robert P. Gillham* was built at Parkersburg, W. Va. in 1901 to tow Campbell's Creek Coal to Louisville.

Nicknamed "Rob'em, Starve'em, Kill'em" by deckhands, the *Gillham* was always kept in the "pink" of condition.

In 1925 the *Gillham* was renamed *Henry C. Yeiser, Jr.* when the Campbell's Creek Coal Company combined with the Hatfield coal interest.

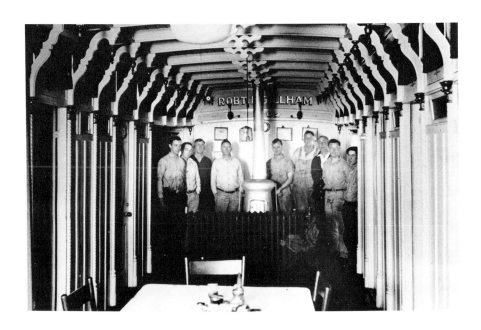

The cabin of the "pride of the Kanawha River" showing her crew. From the left they are: Cecil Faudree, chief engineer; Dexter Melton, cub pilot; Clyde Barnett, mate; Captain Charles M. Young, master; Robert Gibson, striker; Walter Martin, striker; Captain Tom Woodward, pilot; Ralph Horton, second engineer; Sherman Bonecutter, mate.

It was very unusual for the cabin of a towboat to be as ornate as the *Gillham's*. The pride with which the owners and crew held the *Gillham* are clearly evident.

Steamer *Eugene Dana Smith* passing Charleston. Built in 1913 at Dana, W. Va. and named for the grandson of J. B. Dana by the Campbell's Creek Coal Co. The *Smith* towed coal from the Kanawha River to Cincinnati and was rebuilt in 1926.

Dismantled at Reed, W. Va. (new name for Dana) in 1939.

Originally the *Robert P. Gillham* that was built in 1901. Name changed in 1925 by the Hatfield-Campbell's Creek Coal Company interest. Captain Charles Young was her master during the years she was the *Yeiser*. She towed Hatfield-Campbell's Creek largest tow ever to Cincinnati, 28 barges, in June 1936. How the *Yeiser* came to her end is told later in this chapter.

The *Iron Duke* (2nd) was a twin propeller steam tug built at Dana, West Virginia in 1913 for the Campbell's Creek Coal Co. This combination pump-and-tug boat was used at Dana until she was dismantled in 1935 when a new *Iron Duke* was built.

Built at Point Pleasant, West Virginia in 1935, this *Iron Duke* was the third pump boat/tug to carry this name on the Kanawha River. Owned by the Ohio and Kanawha Transportation Co., she was converted to diesel in 1948. Became a part of the Amherst Barge Line Co. in 1951 when the O. & K. Transportation Co. was acquired. Replaced by a diesel towboat of the same name in 1964.

VAL P. COLLINS AND HER CONSTRUCTION CREW
Taken at mouth of Elk River about 1900

Left to right: 1- Si Hill   5- Perry Wright, Supt.
                2- Jeff Thaxton   6- Visitor   9- Tom Gallion
                3- Si Kirk   7- Lou Gleh   10- Geo. Thomas
                4- Unknown   8- Sam Horton   11- W. H. Lynn

The *Val P. Collins* was built at Charleston in 1901 from the towboat *Coal Bluff* which had been built from the towboat *Abe McDonald*. The *McDonald*, built in 1871 was the last steamboat to reach the Kanawha Falls on April 7, 1886. The *Collins* was one of the pioneer towboats for the Island Creek Coal Co. of Huntington, W. Va.

Owned by Collins and Hartweg and used to tow Kanawha River coal to Cincinnati, the *J. B. Lewis* was built in 1900 in just three days less than four months. She was sold south in 1921 where she was lost in a storm in 1926.

The *Reba Reeves* was built at Charleston, W. Va. in 1897. Bought by the Hatfield Coal Co. in March, 1909. She sank in the ice in 1918, was raised and renamed *J. F. Butts*.

Shown in Cincinnati, the *Julius Fleischmann* was operated by the Ohio & Kanawha Transportation Co. and later the Hatfield-Campbell's Creek Line for 25 years. Built as the *Dolphin No. 3* in 1897, then was renamed *Harry Anderson* for two years in 1916 before becoming the *Fleischmann* in 1918. She towed between the Kanawha River and Louisville until she sank in 1945.

Known for it's "wild cat" whistle, the first *J. T. Hatfield* was built in 1904 using the engines from the *Henry De Bus*. Named for Captain J. T. Hatfield, president of the Hickey Transportation Co. of Covington, Kentucky, the *Hatfield* towed Kanawha coal until dismantled in 1930.

Acquired in 1903 by the Hatfield coal interest, the *Henry De Bus* towed Kanawha River coal until dismantled at Pt. Pleasant in 1904. The *De Bus* was built in 1883 at Covington, Kentucky.

Designed for service on the upper Mississippi river and built at Dubuque, Iowa in 1927. The *General Ashburn* was sold to the Ohio & Kanawha Transportation Co. in 1941. Used to tow Kanawha River coal to Cincinnati and Louisville. Sank at Dana, W. Va. on December 24, 1944.

The *General Ashburn* was raised and renamed *J. T. Hatfield* when the Ohio & Kanawha Transportation Co. was absorbed by the Hatfield-Campbell Creek Coal Co. in April 1945. Six years later, the *J. T. Hatfield* (2nd) became a part of the Amherst Barge Co. fleet until sold in 1957 to Armco Steel Corp. who renamed her *Charles R. Hook.*

Built in 1927 for the Federal Barge Line at Dubuque, Iowa and named C. C. *Webber*, the *Ellen Hatfield* was bought by the Ohio & Kanawha Transportation Company in 1947. The name was changed in May 1948 to honor the wife of James T. Hatfield, Sr. by the Hatfield-Campbell Coal Co. Transferred to the Amherst Barge Company in 1953. Dismantled in 1956.

Ellen Hatfield and *Weber W. Sebald* running a staged race on the Kanawha, October 1951.

Built in 1910 at Guild, Tennessee, the *Katherine* was brought to the Kanawha River in 1916 by Pfaff & Smith Builders Supply Co. of Charleston, W. Va. Dismantled in 1930 when the *Joe Cook* was built.

The *Joe Cook* is the first steel hull boat built for the Kanawha River. Built in 1930 for the Pfaff & Smith Builders Supply Co., the *Joe Cook* survived two near disasters to be retired in 1952.

The *F. M. Staunton* and *James Sutherland* of the W. Va. Sand & Gravel Co. work to raise the *Creighton* at Houston, W. Va. in September 1930. The *Creighton* was built from the *Clara Cavett* in 1909 that had been built from the *Mink No. 2* constructed in 1877.

Towing *Edward's Moonlight* excursion barge, the *Creighton* led a parade from Marmet Locks and Dam to Charleston at the 37th Annual Ohio Valley Improvement Association meeting on October 12, 1931.

The highlight of the *F. M. Staunton's* career was towing *Edward's Moonlight* excursion barge with Vice President of the United States Charles Curtis on board at the dedication of Marmet Locks in September 1932. Originally built as the *Winifred* in 1903, this towboat had been named *C. F. Colbert* and *Governor Harding* before becoming the *Staunton* in 1930 by the W. Va. Sand & Gravel Co.

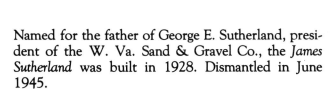

Named for the father of George E. Sutherland, president of the W. Va. Sand & Gravel Co., the *James Sutherland* was built in 1928. Dismantled in June 1945.

Photo courtesy of Dick Sutherland

Originally the packet *Helen E* (See Chapter III) the *Clairmont* was converted from packet to towboat in 1934 by Captain B. D. Raike. He then traded her to showboat owner Billy Bryant for the *Valley Belle*. Sold in 1939, she was used to build a ferry boat.

Built in 1883 as a packet (See Chapter III) the *Valley Belle* ran for 34 years before being sold in 1917 and converted to a towboat. She then continued to operate as a towboat for the next 26 years. The *Valley Belle* ran almost continuously for 60 years without a name change, a unique distinction. She sank in 1943 and was dismantled.

Originally named *H. St. L. Coppee* when built for the Corps of Engineers in 1904. Bought by the Raymond City Coal & Transportation Company in 1935 and renamed *Taric*. Towed Kanawha River coal to Louisville until dismantled in 1947. Captain Harold B. Wright, Jr. earned his master's papers on her in 1942. (See *Kanawha* disaster, Chapter III). He was the great-great grandson of Alexander Wright, pioneer Kanawha River flatboatman; great-grandson of William Penn Wright; (See *Blue Ridge* sinking, Chapter III); grandson of Captain Tom C. Wright, long time pilot on the *Robert P. Gillham* and son of Harold Sr., lockmaster at Ohio River Lock and Dam No. 27. The Wright family's association with the Kanawha River dates back 150 years.

Bought by the Ohio River Dredging Co. in 1931, the *J. C. Rawn* had been named *H. S. Chamberlain* when built in 1911. She carried the name *Weber* briefly when owned by Evansville, Indiana interest.   On December 1, 1939 at Huntington, W. Va., the *J. C. Rawn* exploded two of her three boilers demolishing the boat and killing three men.

In 1943 the *Bessie E. Merrill* was sold to the French government, delivered to Slidell, Louisana, dismantled and sent to the Congo River.

Originally built for the Corps of Engineers and named *General Craighill* in 1911, the *Merrill* was bought by Captain Charles C. Stone in 1939 to do contract towing on the Ohio and Kanawha River. Captain Stone renamed her *Bessie E. Merrill*.

Captain Charles C. Stone bought the Corps of Engineers towboat *Merrill*, originally built in 1907, in 1931. He renamed her *Tu-Endi-We* after the point where the Kanawha River meets the Ohio River. She was used for contract towing on those two rivers until dismantled in 1943.

The A. C. *Ingersoll, Jr.* was built in 1923 and originally named *Robert Taylor.* Her name was changed to W. T. Smoot and *Convoy* before being bought by the Philadelphia & Cleveland Coal Company in 1923 who changed her name to A. C. *Ingersoll, Jr.* She towed coal out of the Kanawha River and from Huntington for the Ohio River Company. She was destroyed by fire in August 1940.

Built at Charleston, W. Va. in 1925 for the Ohio River Company, the *E. D. Kenna* worked on the Mississippi, Ohio, Kanawha and Illinois Rivers during her career. She was taken to Pittsburgh in 1952 and traded in for a diesel replacement boat, the *Lucy Jane Lucas.* Dismantled in 1953.

The *Omar* was built in 1936 for the Ohio River Company of Cincinnati. In 1939 she took 28 barges of coal, a total of 22,792 tons, from Huntington to Cincinnati in a single trip. A feat not attempted since the wooden coal boat days.

She was decommissioned in 1961 and in 1962, remodeled into a museum/showboat theater by the State of West Virginia as a part of their centennial celebration. Renamed *Rhododendron*, she was towed along the state's waterways from Charleston to Fairmont. Sold to the city of Clinton, Iowa in 1966 who renamed her *Showboat* and used as a tourist attraction.

Built at Point Pleasant, W. Va. in 1940 by the Marietta Manufacturing Co., the Union Barge Line named the boat *Jason* when they bought it in 1941. The name was changed to *Herbert E. Jones* in 1951 after being bought by the Hatfield-Campbell Creek Coal Co. The *Jones* was the last large sternwheel steam towboat to operate on the Kanawha. The last owner of the *Jones* was the Amherst Industries, Inc. of Port Amherst (Charleston) which is owned by the Jones family. Decommissioned in 1961, the 25 foot diameter sternwheel from the *Jones* is now a permanent display at Station Square in Pittsburgh.

The *Junior* was originally named *Lieut. Gurney* when built at Dubuque, Iowa in 1911. Bought by the Raymond City Coal and Transportation Company in 1936 and renamed *Junior*. Sold and dismantled in 1984.

The varied use of steam at Cabin Creek on the Kanawha about 1940

The *Slack Barrett* pushes a tow of empty barges east toward Montgomery past the Cabin Creek Electric Power Plant.

Named for Captain Slack Barrett, a prominent member of a family long associated with riverboats, this towboat had the distinction of bearing the same name twice during her career. In 1922 she was sold to the U.S. Army Corps of Engineers who renamed her *Tuscumbia* and used her on the Tennessee River. In 1939, she was bought by the Ohio River Dredging Company at Huntington who gave her back her original name, *Slack Barrett* which she retained until she was retired and dis-

mantled in 1949.

By coincidence the Cabin Creek Power Plant, a pioneer in the steam generation of electricity, was built the same year as the *Slack Barrett*—1914.

All of this scene is now only history except for the mountains and the river.

Steamboat Description and Construction

My first day on the river was spent making an inventory, laboriously listing the contents of E.A.'s (Captain E. A. Burnside, general manager of the Campbell's Creek Coal Co.) storeroom of steamboat supplies, most of which were unfamiliar to me. "Win" helped me over the rough spots. "What's this?" I would ask him, holding out an article of hardware. "That's a drift bolt," he would explain and laugh. "And that is a barge spike." By evening my vocabulary was a maze of new terms and I was very alive in the fact that steamboats were constructed of strakes, futtocks, carlins, cod-wads, and fantails. So many odd things! "Win" blandly explained with appropriate gestures how to distinguish a male from a female syphon coupling. I blushed at this rare and priceless disclosure and nominated the rat tail bastard file as being the most honest and appropriately named instrument in the collection.

Pilotin' Comes Natural
Frederick Way, Jr.
1943

(used by permission of the author)

The *Gene Dana* was typical of hundreds of steamboats plying the Mississippi River and its tributaries: she was known as "pool boat" type which, in river parlance, means the pilothouse was built forward of the cabin on the second deck, and not on top of it. She was a sternwheeler, was designed to push barges and do sundry menial work, was not equipped for passengers nor did she ever carry any freight on her decks—very much the same as a tug in oceanwise service save that she never pulled barges behind her. All of the barges on western streams are gathered into a unit, securely lashed together with rope and wire, and the towboat is hitched to the rear of the mass and shores it. "Towboat" is one of those idiotic terms on the western streams which does not mean what the word infers: the *Gene Dana* and her kin were not towboats; they were pushboats. A western boatman will only look at you in bewilderment if you speak of pushboats, however; he pushes with a towboat. The *Gene Dana* was 121 feet long, not counting her paddlewheel which sprawled perhaps twenty additional feet to the rear, and she was 26 feet wide. You could wade in water she floated in and not get your pants pockets wet. Her hull was so extremely shallow that the deck, built on it, was perhaps four inches out of the water amidship and a careless pilot one time pulled the rudders hard over to miss a cake of floating ice and the boat careened to a precarious angle, darted for shore, straightened up, and when everybody had recovered his breath there was a block or river ice lodged in the engine room (not the one she swerved to avoid, but a close relative: both came from the Allegheny River). This boat was interesting in other ways.

The low deck built on top of the hull served as the floor for the engines and boilers and most of the equipment which had to do with her business of towing barges. The second deck, called the "boiler deck" (and never, since the inception of the western steamboat did it ever have a boiler on it) was made up into living quarters for the crew—this boat ran day and night and there had to be two pilots, two engineers, two mates, two firemen and two sets of deckhands: two of everybody save the cook and cabin help. These persons took turns sleeping in small rooms provided with upper and lower bunks and equipped just like a passenger boat. The pilothouse was built on the forward end of the cabin and could be entered from inside. Ahead of the pilothouse the twin smokestacks jutted through the boiler deck and went aloft about ten feet higher than the top of the pilothouse. This general scheme of construction was not thought up by a drunken man; on the contrary it was perfected to suit the particular needs of shallow river navigation and the *Gene Dana* and her brethren were as much at home on the Kanawha River as the *Queen Mary* is upon the sea.

Pilotin' Comes Natural
Captain Fredrick Way, Jr.
1943

(used by permission of the author)

The towboat *Otto Marmet* ran on the Kanawha River from 1898 to 1935. Her original hull was built on the banks of the Pocatalico River, a Kanawha tributary, at Raymond City, W. Va.

The following photographs show the building of the hull and it launching. All but the last photograph are from the Herschel Burford Collection, West Virginia State Archives.

October 13, 1897. All of the ribs are in place shaping the hull and revealing both it's shallow draft and model bow. Most towboat hulls were built with model bows. At the stern, three rudder posts are clearly seen.

The hull is now almost boarded up and the deck support timbers are in place. Steam is rising from a hot water vat into which the wood was placed to make it pliable so it could be shaped.

The hog chain braces are in place and the sternwheel support timbers are set on the deck. At the bow the gallows frame is set and ready to support a tall jack staff.

The hog chain braces will support the hog chains and (See photo No. 5) act as a truss support system for the hull after the boilers and engines are installed.

Launching day and a crowd gathers. The towing knee support are now in place and the hog chains have been attached. Note small boat name sign on upright support near the bow.

November 27, 1897. One of the great thrills of a launching was to be permitted to ride the hull into the river. The launching of the *Otto Marmet* drew a number of riders including a few women.

When the *Otto Marmet* was launched her hull was only 128.6 feet long by 28.3 feet wide. She was later lengthened to 142.5 feet long as seen here, bringing empties back to the Kanawha River.

The River Giveth — The River Taketh Away

A great river at full flood is a fearful thing to see. Neither man nor his works are an equal to the power of nature.

The drama that unfolded on August 15, 1940 began with a cloudburst along the Virginia-West Virginia border. Soon the Greenbrier, Bluestone and New Rivers passed their ever rising waters to the Great Kanawha and this was the force that would bring about the destruction of a veteran Kanawha River towboat.

The *Henry C. Yeiser*, as any old hand would tell you was really none other than the *Robert P. Gilliam*. She had been renamed *Yeiser* but was the same boat that had plied the Great Kanawha since 1901.

In August 1940 she was laid up on the riverbank in the landing of the Hatfield-Campbells Creek Coal Co. at Reed (now Amherst) a short ways up the river from Charleston. Her huge paddlewheel had been removed for repair and she was due to be back at work soon.

The flood tide struck a fleet of floating equip-ment at Alloy, above Montgomery and swept several barges from their moorings. This floating battering ram soon reached the *Yeiser* at Reed and with the force of hundreds of tons of steel driven by thousands of tons of water the venerable old towboat was thrust into the rushing river along with the smaller steam towboat, *J. F. Butts*.

The *Butts* was to survive the ordeal that followed escaping disaster by a mere few feet. Word quickly spread across Charleston that a great fleet of equipment was on its way downstream, unmaned and out of control.

Photographers raced to the riverbank in anticipation of the scenes that were to unfold.

The *Yeiser* and the *Butts* somehow passed safely between the piers of both the Kanawha City and the South Side Bridges. By the time they had cleared the mouth of the Elk River, the suspense continued to mount as awestruck spectators followed down the boulevard; in cars, on foot, on bicycles, young and old alike.

The old C & O Bridge loomed ahead, not far below the Elk and it was there that luck ran out for the *Yeiser*.

The thrust of the Elk's flow into the Kanawha directed the fleet over toward the south bank and straight into the south piers of the bridge.

There was a universal holding of breath as all hoped against hope that the old boat might make it through. With a sickening crash the *Yeiser* smashed into the concrete pier. Fate seem to rule against her as the point of impact was near the center of her hull. Instead of simply spinning around the pier, she was hung up as the unending force of the on rushing river continued to beat against her starboard side. The *O.K. #5*, a derrick barge, then slammed into the *Yeiser*, capsized and was reduced to splinters. For a few moments the game old towboat withstood the incredible onslaught, but then she began to tip over until her deck caught the full force of the tide.

We mortals seem to love the vessels we create, almost as if they are somehow alive, possessing a spirit. This old boat was like a good friend, so familiar to everyone up and down the Great Kanawha from Point Pleasant to Montgomery. For 39 years she had served faithfully bearing her burden of coal to light and heat the nation's cities.

Now she was dying—in full view of all so familiar with her by both sight and sound.

There would be no rescue this day; no pumping out, no rebuilding. This was the end, stark and final. Relentlessly the river drew her down. Desperate sounds echoed across the water, breaking glass, splintering wood and the groan of her collapsing hull.

What memories of the familiar old *Henry C. Yeiser, Jr.* came rushing back to the minds of the onlookers as she capsized and disappeared beneath the flood waters?... her melodious whistle echoing off the city building and hills; trying to catch a wave from her paddle-wheel in a canoe or rowboat; just being transfixed by the reflecting moonlight as it sparkled from the splash of the sternwheel on a summer night?

The *J. F. Butts* made it safely through and was caught by *Pfaff & Smith* workers on downstream. She was later dismantled in 1942.

The old railroad bridge still stands exactly as it was on that morning over half a century ago. Thousands of people pass by every day little knowing that one of the last steamboats on the Kanawha died there.

Although many have tried to locate and retrieve the big brass whistle that those who lived on the valley had come to know and love, it stays on the bottom of the river. Another of the secrets of the Great Kanawha.

As the fleet of run-away vessels nears the bridge, the *Yeiser* strikes the pier. The derrick boat *O. and K. No. 5* heads directly for the *Yeiser*.

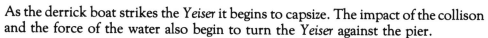
As the derrick boat strikes the *Yeiser* it begins to capsize. The impact of the collison and the force of the water also begin to turn the *Yeiser* against the pier.

As the water washes over the *Yeiser's* deck, she begins to roll beneath the surface pinned against the pier.

The *Henry C. Yeiser, Jr.* sinks under the waters of the Kanawha River where she had worked for 39 years.

"Let's Catch Her!"

Dan Petersen and his brother Joe had gone up to their father's boat dock to see if the rampaging Kanawha River was causing any damage. Both the boys had grown up around the river and their father, a prominent Charleston physician, owned a boat club near South Ruffner just west of the Kanawha City Bridge. It was summer and the teenagers were living a carefree life awaiting the start of school.

Dan remembered the bad flood of 1937 and on this August day of 1940 he knew what a raging river could do. When the youngsters arrived at the boat dock their eyes were met with an astonishing sight. Out in the middle of the rushing torrent they saw the 150 foot towboat *Henry C. Yeiser* drifting stern first under the Kanawha City Bridge. It didn't take the boys long to figure out that no one was on board and that the familiar old boat was out of control. Quickly they decided to try to board her—not so much with any plan in mind but simply as a devil may care stunt! Doctor Petersen kept a 15 foot metal lifeboat that had come off of the old steamboat *Unique*. The lively inboard motor had been fitted and the sturdy little craft was just right for the job.

As they shoved off into the rushing stream Dan noticed that the motor's propeller often struck floating debris but they went ahead with the confidence that only youth can muster. Dan estimated the flood tide was flowing over ten miles an hour but since they were not going upstream the looming hulk of the *Yeiser* was not too difficult to catch.

With their imaginations running wild, the two daring youngsters leaped onto the derelicts deck and tied up their small craft. Swiftly they raced through the big towboat to see if anyone was aboard.

Dan recalled the scene that confronted him in the glass enclosed pilothouse: "Everything was perfectly in order and I'll never forget a beautiful pair of binoculars hanging on the wall." The two brothers paused for a moment to debate their situation and try to devise some way to save the *Yeiser*. The river gave them a grim foreboding of possible disaster and they decided to return to their motorboat and leave the unfortunate stern-wheeler to her fate. It is very probable that this decision saved their lives. Soon after the *Yeiser* passed safely beneath the South Side Bridge and near the city levee they cast off and made their way close to the south bank. In order to avoid drifting debris they headed their tiny craft upstream directly atop the submerged lower sidewalk of the Kanawha Boulevard which was now about three feet under water.

It was all the small motor could do to make any progress back toward the dock at South Ruffner.

The brothers could hardly have imagined the fate of the *Yeiser* or that she had only a few more minutes of existence.

Later that day of course, they heard that the big towboat had struck the C & O Railroad Bridge and had sunk violently after capsizing less than ten minutes after they had left her.

It is safe to say that these boys had flirted with death that August 15th, half a century ago.

Dan Petersen related this story on September 7, 1990. He is still a resident of Charleston, retired from Union Carbide after a long career as a Mechanical Engineer. In his life he has done many exciting things including service as a fighter pilot during World War II but as he recalled that madcap adventure on the flooding Kanawha River, his eyes lit up and you could almost see him as a spry 15-year-old scrambling onto the deck of the *Henry C. Yeiser!*

Kanawha River Steam Towboat
— Circa 1947 —

The steamer *O. F. Shearer* was owned and operated by O. F. Shearer & Sons of Cedar Grove, W. Va.

She was originally named *Victory* when built at Dravo Corporation, Neville Island, Pennsylvania in 1919.

Acquired by the Shearers in 1940 who changed her name and towed coal from the Kanawha River to Cincinnati until 1951, when she was retired and dismantled.

The following pages illustrate life on a towboat which was a workplace and home for a "family" for many days.

The *Shearer* was a "pool type" towboat with her pilot house forward of the cabin. She had short smoke stacks hinged with heavy counterweights to assist in lowering them if necessary to pass under bridges.

Captain Bert Shearer stands his watch—six hours on and six hours off—seven days a week. Recalls the captain: "She was a good handler but a poor backer."

Master of all he surveys, Captain William "Bill" Curry guides the *Shearer* and tow down the Kanawha.

An old veteran of the steam era—Curry once took a yawl from Pt. Pleasant to Cincinnati at low water, before locks and dams, in order to observe and mark the channel.

The pilot wheel from this photo is now in the West Virginia Culture Center.

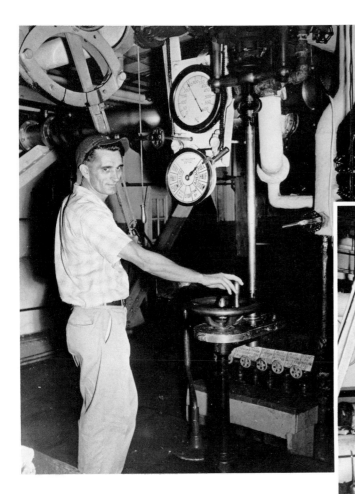

Chief Engineer Lewis Faudree stands ready to respond to orders from the pilot house, hand on throttle, ever mindful of steam pressure guage.

Stricker Howard "Pat" Patterson in front of the electric circuitboard. A stricker was an apprentice engineer. The clock now hangs in Captain Bert Shearer's den.

Alert to both the engine room telegraph and steam pressure gauge, Second Engineer James Casto began his watch.

James Casto stands next to reversing lever while his helper, Meese Snodgrass, is ready with the ever present oil can and rag. Heat in the engine room was intense in the summer; welcomed in the winter.

Fireman Watson shakes the grates to clear away the burnt coal.

Deck hands rest against the Bitts near the bow of the *Shearer*. The rope to signal the pilothouse that a tow had been cut loose is seen between men on right.

Roast beef and fresh baked pies were just two of Mrs. "Moody" Williamson's specialties. Remembered as a "top cook," she later worked on the *Duncan Bruce*.

Cook helper sets table for "family-style" supper. Dining rooms were run in "spic and span" order.

Boat owners knew that a well fed crew was a content crew so great pains were taken to set a good table. Maid Virginia Williamson serves drinks to (l. to r.) Chief Engineer Lewis Faudree, Steersman Paul Ruttencutter, Striker Howard "Pat" Patterson and Captain Bert Shearer.

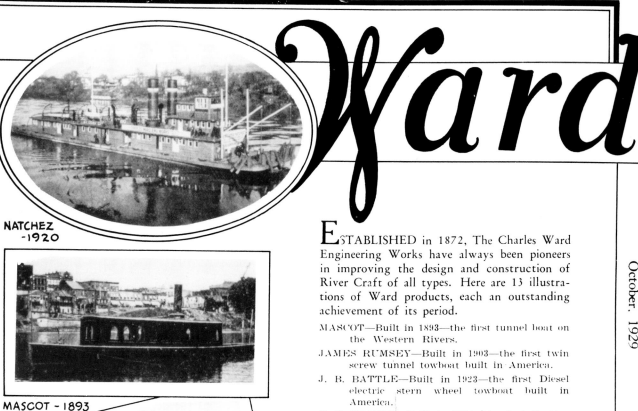

Ward

NATCHEZ -1920

MASCOT - 1893

ESTABLISHED in 1872, The Charles Ward Engineering Works have always been pioneers in improving the design and construction of River Craft of all types. Here are 13 illustrations of Ward products, each an outstanding achievement of its period.

MASCOT—Built in 1893—the first tunnel boat on the Western Rivers.

JAMES RUMSEY—Built in 1903—the first twin screw tunnel towboat built in America.

J. B. BATTLE—Built in 1923—the first Diesel electric stern wheel towboat built in America.

C. B. HARRIS—Built in 1924—the first Suction Dredge, with direct Diesel engine driven pump, built for River service.

DUNCAN BRUCE—Built in 1929—the largest and most powerful stern wheel towboat with direct Diesel drive.

JAMES RUMSEY -1903

J. B. BATTLE -1923

DWIGHT F. DAVIS -1929

GEO. T. PRICE - 1925

W. A. SHEPARD -1927

THE CHARLES WARD
DESIGNERS AND BUILDERS OF RIVER CRAFT OF ALL TYPES

Leadership

GEORGE T. HARRIS (1925); W. A. SHEPARD, (1927); INCOR, (1928). The first three twin screw tunnel towboats of 720 h.p., each equipped with Diesel engines.

DWIGHT F. DAVIS—Built in 1929—the first vessel actually designed and built to use pulverized coal under its boilers.

TWO TOWBOATS—Twin screw tunnel towboats with Turbo-Electric drive—the first of their type—building for the Standard Unit Navigation Company.

WHITE SWAN—The largest modern passenger vessel designed and proposed for Western River service.

GEN. FRANK M. COXE and GEN. JOHN McE. HYDE—Built in 1922—the first twin screw passenger vessels built on the rivers for ocean-going service.

NATCHEZ—Built in 1920—the first of a fleet of 2000 h.p., twin screw tunnel towboats.

INCOR - 1928

GEN. FRANK M. COXE -1922

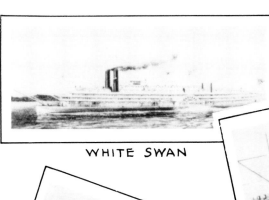

WHITE SWAN

SUNCO

DUNCAN BRUCE 1927

C. B. HARRIS - 1924

ENGINEERING WORKS
CHARLESTON, WEST VIRGINIA

The scene above occurred on Saturday, March 7, 1903 on the Kanawha River a short distance above Charleston. The small propeller-driven boat is the new Charles Ward Engineering Company's *James Rumsey* going head-to-head in a staged pushing contest with the "cock-of-the-walk" of Kanawha River towboats, *D. T. Lane*. The results of this contest was to signal the beginning of the end of sternwheel riverboats. Details of this action are provided on the next two pages.

This contest was the culmination of Charles Ward's efforts to prove his boilers and propeller boats.

Charles Ward emigrated to Cincinnati from Southam, England in 1870. The following year he moved to Charleston to assist in the installation of the first gas plant in the Kanawha valley.

In 1872, Ward started his own business and in 1878 he built his first boiler for the *Wild Goose* (1st) for Dr. J. P. Hale. The success of this and

other boilers led to the building of the Charles Ward Engineering Company on the south side of the Kanawha River across form the center of downtown Charleston, W. Va.

Ward built boilers that were considered to be the world's best by many marine designers. 400 Ward boilers were ordered by the Navy and other government departments during World War I. In addition to the boilers, Ward pioneered the tunnel-type propeller light draft boat for inland river navigation.

The largest vessel built by Ward was the 286-foot long steam railroad car ferry steamer *St. Genevieve* in 1922. This vessel had a capacity for 21 freight cars on a single trip.

Although the Ward Engineering Company ceased production in the early 1930's, many of it's boats are still operating today. Two of these boats still run the Kanawha River; they are the *P. A. Denny* and the *Major*.

Charleston Daily Gazette, March 8, 1903.

JAMES RUMSEY TRIUMPHANT
MODERN ENGINEERING EXCELS

The New Government Tug Has Successfully Withstood All Tests.

And Was Victorious in Yesterday's Pushing Contest With the Lane.

Description of This Latest Specimen of Boat Builder's Ingenuity.

More than five thousand Charleston people witnessed an exhibition on Saturday of the triumph of modern and scientific steamboat building in the contest of the relative power possessed by the tow boat D. T. Lane, owned by the Campbell's Creek Coal company, one of the best known of the Kanawha river craft, and the James Rumsey, the United States Government's newly completed twin screw propeller, which was built entirely at the Ward Engineering works, in Charleston, and which is to take the place of the steamer Bee, which has been condemned and gone out of service.

Since the completion of the James Rumsey that craft has undergone many peculiar and novel tests. She is built on lines entirely new to engineering skill in the western waters, and like all advances in science, had been subjected to the skepticism of the laymen as well as the doubts and objections of the old line steamboat engineers and river men. The Rumsey is a twin screw propeller with quadruple expansion engines. That means that the steam generated for the motive power is used four times through cylinders of 7, 10, 14 and 20 inches in diameter, that alone being a triumph of mechanical skill most noteworthy and valuable in this line of business. She is 120 feet long, has a 22 foot beam, depth of hull 4 feet 6 inches, all of which is steel. She has an average draught of 28 inches, and a required speed of 12 miles an hour.

The speed requirement was the first feature of the Rumsey to outstrip the expectations of the builders. On her first trip out and before the installation of one or two perfecting features she made thirteen and one-third miles an hour and thus prominence as to speed was established. The horse-power of her engines is 450, the steam for which is generated in one of the Ward upright boilers, already well known in the steamboat world. In the construction of the Rumsey the ingenuity of the builders stand out in most prominence. The engines, boiler and all the vital machinery of the craft are located directly in the center of the boat, the coal being stored in invisible bunkers along the sides.

Entering from the bow is a large office for the captain, with state room, bathroom, lavatory, and private apartment. At the stern is the kitchen, dining room and sleeping apartments for the remainder of the crew, with the same personal conveniences as are noted in the bow. Every detail of convenience seems to have been studied in the construction of the craft, and she appears to the observer as a model of ingenuity and convenience.

As has been said the Rumsey has been subjected to almost every known test of practicability since her completion. She has had all the paraphernalia of the Government property in the Kanawha lashed to her sides, and has swung them up and down the river, across and back to the banks, landed, swung around in midstream with all these encumbrances, and through all stood her tests with remarkable firmness and ease.

But it remained for the builder of the craft to put the Rumsey to a test of strength and power which few would have had the temerity to have proposed. Mr. Chas. Ward, the senior of the firm of builders, proposed that the Rumsey enter into a contest for a test of strength with the D. T. Lane, one of the very best, most reliable and strongest towboats plying the Kanawha river. Practically all experienced steamboatmen were astounded at the proposition made by the Wards. They gave the Rumsey credit for being a marvel in convenience, stable and able for her requirements, but in a strength test with the D. T. Lane she would be a pigmy in the hands of a giant. But the Wards believed they could show their faith by the works of the Rumsey, so when it was insisted that the Rumsey be accommodated with an opportunity, the owners of the boat gave their consent, and Saturday about ten o'clock the Lane came in from above with a tow of barges, lashed them to the bank near the big bridge, and stood out in the stream, big, square built and imposing, as if to invite the diminutive steel hulled model of the evolution that is taking place in western waters to come on for the sacrifice.

The Rumsey was not long in coming across. She had been moored on the South Side near the Ward works, and when it appeared that all arrangements were complete she whirled slowly and evenly out into the river, executed a swing or two, just to show the big antagonist that she was not afraid, and then came smoothly up and stuck her nose against the prow of her gigantic antagonist.

Captain Patrick was in charge of the Lane, and was assisted in the test by Captain Summerfield. The fact that these two well known and competent steamboatmen were in command of the Lane meant beyond all doubt that the Rumsey would be required to show all the spunk in her if she won in the apparently unequal contest.

It was announced that the Lane was in the primest condition. She had had a good trip, her four hundred and fifty horse-power was not hampered at any part, and her crew were working like the parts of a well timed watch. She is about three times the weight of the Rumsey, her horse power the same and government requirement as to steam about the same as the contesting craft. Her engine cylinders are sixteen inches in diameter with a five foot and a half stroke. There wasn't an imperfect feature in the Lane's makeup and she looked fit for any reasonable contest.

As soon as the prows of the two boats had been fastened securely together, and they stood out in the water just below the first big pier of the bridge, the thousands who had assembled on the levee and from the windows of the buildings along the river had a fine opportunity to note the tremendous disparity in the sizes of the two craft. The Lane towered above the Rumsey like a Goliah. But the little boat sat square on her bottom and her appearance inspired a degree of confidence in some who watched intently the preparations for a vital contest which would mark the passing of the old craft and the coming of the new and modern power.

When lashed together, the two boats stood out in the water, the Lane being on the upper side. This gave the Lane the current, the wind, which was rather stiff at the time, as well as the advantage offered by being within direct range of the bridge pier. The little Rumsey had nothing in its favor. At a given signal the engines sprang to work. The ponderous wheel of the Lane began to revolve with tremendous power. All that could indicate that the Rumsey was doing anything to resist the awful force of the big towboat was a whirr of her smoothly running machinery and a swirling of the water toward the rear of the craft. Presently the Rumsey began to perceptibly move down stream. The Lane puffed, her big wheel whirled with awful force, throwing great fragments of water in the air. The Rumsey was moving against the almost resistless force. Captain Jim Martin, of the Calderwood, who was intently watching the contest from the deck of the Rumsey, noted that the Rumsey was being pushed not quite so fast as the current. This situation continued until the boats reached a point at the west limit of the city levee. Then a signal was given and power on both craft was shut off. The boats stopped dead still.

At a given signal the power of both was again turned on. There was a shuddering sensation on board the Rumsey, the Lane roared with her fires; like a mighty giant she struggled a moment and then began to slowly but surely move back up the stream. The Rumsey had asserted her power! She had conquered the giant towboat and was pushing her up the stream again all the power and force that could be driven from a great wheel and ponderous engine. When she had pushed the Lane a distance of about sixty feet, all hands signaled off, and there was a stop.

Hundreds were amazed that the Lane should have pushed the Rumsey the distance noted, and then in turn be started back a moment later. Experts on board the Rumsey and Lane gave this explanation: When the

start was made the current, wind, and the break-water of the pier were tremendously in favor of the big boat. In addition the fireman of the Rumsey was unable to raise steam to a proper pressure. With all these handicaps it was surprising that the first stage of the contest was not a walkaway for the big boat.

Following this trial the boats then reversed, the Lane taking the lower side, while the Rumsey swung up stream. Three separate tests were made while in this position, in all of which the Rumsey slowly but surely bore the big boat down the stream. Then the test was reversed and backing contest was tried. In this the Rumsey showed to much better advantage than in the pushing contest, and with apparent ease carried the Lane with her up the stream for some distance.

In the beginning of the contest there was but little enthusiasm displayed by the thousands of people who lined the banks, as it was evident that almost the entire populace assembled had their sympathies with the little boat. But when the little wonder rounded out to her real form, and began sending her big antagonist almost at will, the crowd appreciated the fact that her superiority was established and the air was soon filled with the huzzas of the crowd, and the crew on board the little craft received many encouraging cheers.

Mr. Charles Ward, the senior of the firm, as well as his two sons, Messrs. Charles E. and Harold, were on the Rumsey during the entire time of the test and watched every feature of the test with intense interest and noted every movement of the two boats. At its close the elder Mr. Ward expressed his entire satisfaction as well as gratification and declared that the Rumsey had done no more than he had expected, knowing so well and so thoroughly her qualities and build.

A representative of the Gazette was in the company of Captain Jim Martin of the Calderwood, on the Rumsey most of the time during the test of strength. Captain Martin watched the work of the boat with a critical eye, noted every movement she made, and at the finish was loud in his praise of the wonderful work of the vessel. When the boats cut loose, and Pilot Johnson, of the Rumsey, had been relieved, Captain Martin went into the pilot house, took the wheel and the Rumsey was given her nose for a whirl up and down the river at her best pace. Captain Martin turned her with the ease almost of a duck, and as she came skimming back past the levee her big fog-horn whistle was let loose and the thousands of spectators on the banks gave her a joyous reception. Mr. Charles E. Ward, assisted by Capt. Dryden, ran up a new broom at the masthead, denoting the victory of the Rumsey, and one of the most memorable events in the history of Charleston was ended.

This exhibition of the Rumsey is of most far-reaching importance to Charleston, as well as to the builders and owners of the great plant here that bears their name. It establishes beyond all doubt the superiority of this class of vessels for towing purposes, and is convincing proof that the days of the big and expensive towboat are numbered. It also cheapens the cost of navigation to one-third and will enable boats to ply in less water than formerly. The Wards are to be congratulated on their achievements and Charleston should feel a just pride in claiming them as citizens.

The packet *Katydid* was fitted with the second Ward boiler made. She originally ran between Charleston and Gallipolis and brought the Cincinnati daily papers to Charleston on the day of issue. The *Katydid* was known for her swiftness and her economy of fuel consumption.

Advertisement used by the Ward Engineering Company to announce the success of its boiler for ocean vessels.

The launching of the *Indiana* on June 16, 1930. The *Indiana* was the first river towboat to have a steam turbo-electric drive. This was among the last Ward built boats.

Ward Engineering Co. - 1921
The river steam towboat *Destrehan* and the *U.S.S. General Frank M. Coxe* and *General John McE. Hyde* nearing completion. This photograph illustrates the distinct difference between the construction of riverboats and ocean going vessels.

Built in 1930 by the Ward Engineering Works, the *Scott* towed for the Corps of Engieers until 1954. She was brought back to the Kanawha River in 1973 and converted into a private launch named *Robin D. Too.* Later converted into an excursion boat and renamed *P. A. Denny*, she now operates out of Charleston, W. Va.

Ward's invisioned luxury passenger steamboat, *White Swan.* Had she been built, she would have been the marvel of the Mississippi River for size alone.

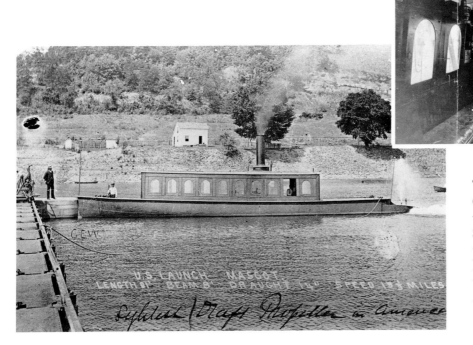

The *Mascot* was built by Charles Ward in 1893 for the Corps of Engineers. She was used as an inspection boat on the Kanawha River. Later used as a private launch by Captain E. A. Burnside.

In 1925, Ward Engineering Company built the *George T. Price*. The *Price* was the first twin-propeller diesel towboat built.

Kanawha River Sternwheel Legacy

When 13-year old Nelson Jones went to Charleston, W. Va. Mayor John Hutchinson in 1971 and suggested holding a sternwheel boat race on the Kanawha River, neither could have foreseen what this event would develop into.

The first Charleston Sternwheel Regatta had five sternwheel boats in the race. The boats were the *Winnie Mae*, Captain Harry White; *Robin D.*, P. A. (Pete) Denny, owner - Captain Bert Shearer, pilot; *Laura J.*, Charles T. Jones; *Momma Jeanne*, Lawson Hamilton and *Claire E.*, Captain Gene Fitch. The little *Katydid* owned by Clifford Dean was present but did not participate.

The *Winnie Mae* won this first contest and with this win set into motion the 1972 sternwheel race. Each successive year has seen the Charleston Sternwheel Regatta grow into a week long festival including a wide variety of events culminating with the sternwheel races. The sternwheel races are held on the Labor Day weekend before crowds numbering in the thousands.

Today two excursion boats operate on the Kanawha River on a regular basis.

The *West Virginia Belle* is a diesel-propeller excursion/dinner cruise boat with a non-operative sternwheel. She operates on both the Kanawha and Ohio Rivers year 'round providing day long trips between Charleston and Huntington, W. Va. as well as day and evening excursions at both locations.

The *P. A. Denny* was originally named *Scott* and built at the Charles Ward Engineering Company at Charleston, W. Va. in 1930 (See Chapter 6). She was completely re-built in 1973 as a private pleasure craft before being converted into an excursion boat in 1976. A true sternwheeler, the *Denny* runs excursion in the Charleston area and is available for private parties and special events.

The *P. A. Denny* at Charleston, W. Va. during America's 1976 Bicentennial Celebration. Built originally as the *Scott* at Charles Ward Engineering Co., Charleston, W. Va., 1930.

1989 Charleston Sternwheel Regatta.

The *Major* was built at Charleston, W. Va. in 1928 at Charles Ward Engineering Co. Today she is owned by Captain Nelson Jones of Amherst Ltd., Charleston, W. Va.

Providing both Kanawha and Ohio River excursions, the *West Virginia Belle* is known for its' prime rib dinner cruises.

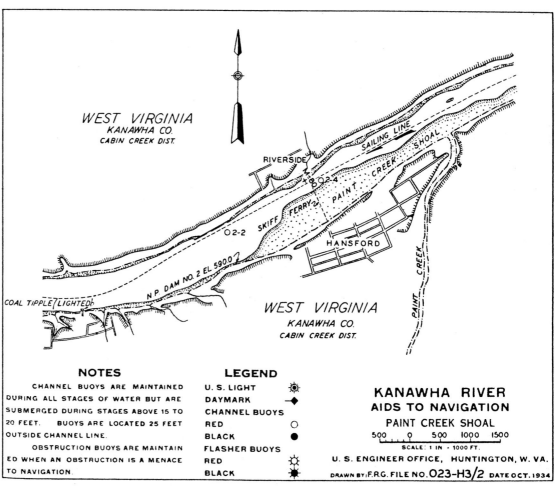

WEST VIRGINIA
KANAWHA CO.
CABIN CREEK DIST.

RIVERSIDE

SKIFF FERRY

PAINT CREEK SHOAL

SAILING LINE

O 2-2

HANSFORD

N.P. DAM NO. 2 EL 590.0

COAL TIPPLE (LIGHTED)

WEST VIRGINIA
KANAWHA CO.
CABIN CREEK DIST.

PAINT CREEK

NOTES

CHANNEL BUOYS ARE MAINTAINED DURING ALL STAGES OF WATER BUT ARE SUBMERGED DURING STAGES ABOVE 15 TO 20 FEET. BUOYS ARE LOCATED 25 FEET OUTSIDE CHANNEL LINE.

OBSTRUCTION BUOYS ARE MAINTAINED WHEN AN OBSTRUCTION IS A MENACE TO NAVIGATION.

LEGEND

U.S. LIGHT	☀
DAYMARK	◆
CHANNEL BUOYS	
RED	○
BLACK	●
FLASHER BUOYS	
RED	☼
BLACK	✺

KANAWHA RIVER
AIDS TO NAVIGATION
PAINT CREEK SHOAL

500   0   500   1000   1500
SCALE: 1 IN. = 1000 FT.

U. S. ENGINEER OFFICE, HUNTINGTON, W. VA.

DRAWN BY: F.R.G. FILE NO. 023-H3/2 DATE OCT. 1934

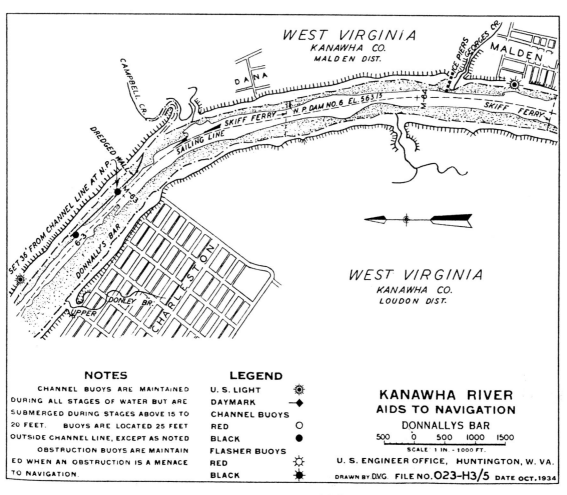

WEST VIRGINIA
KANAWHA CO.
MALDEN DIST.

CAMPBELL CR.

DANA

ICE PIERS

ST. GEORGES CR.

MALDEN

SKIFF FERRY

N.P. DAM NO. 6 EL 563.15

M-64

SKIFF FERRY

SAILING LINE

DREDGED TO CHANNEL LINE AT N.P.

M-63

SET 36' FROM CHANNEL LINE AT N.P.

6-3

DONNALLY'S BAR

DONLEY BR.

UPPER

CHARLESTON

WEST VIRGINIA
KANAWHA CO.
LOUDON DIST.

NOTES

CHANNEL BUOYS ARE MAINTAINED DURING ALL STAGES OF WATER BUT ARE SUBMERGED DURING STAGES ABOVE 15 TO 20 FEET. BUOYS ARE LOCATED 25 FEET OUTSIDE CHANNEL LINE, EXCEPT AS NOTED

OBSTRUCTION BUOYS ARE MAINTAINED WHEN AN OBSTRUCTION IS A MENACE TO NAVIGATION.

LEGEND

U. S. LIGHT	☀
DAYMARK	◆
CHANNEL BUOYS	
RED	○
BLACK	●
FLASHER BUOYS	
RED	☼
BLACK	✺

KANAWHA RIVER
AIDS TO NAVIGATION
DONNALLYS BAR

500   0   500   1000   1500
SCALE: 1 IN. = 1000 FT.

U. S. ENGINEER OFFICE, HUNTINGTON, W. VA.

DRAWN BY: D.V.G. FILE NO. 023-H3/5 DATE OCT. 1934

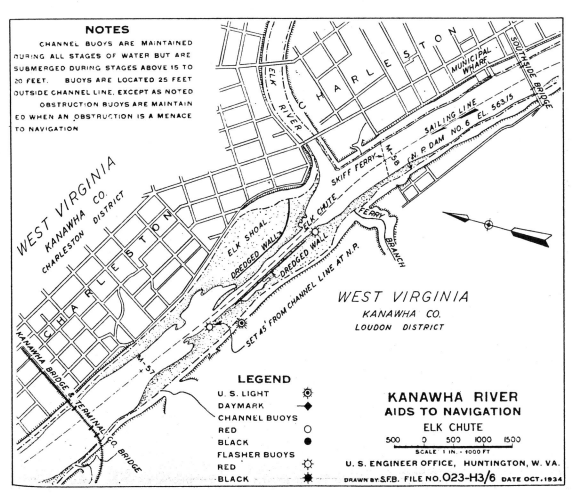

NOTES

CHANNEL BUOYS ARE MAINTAINED DURING ALL STAGES OF WATER BUT ARE SUBMERGED DURING STAGES ABOVE 15 TO 20 FEET.   BUOYS ARE LOCATED 25 FEET OUTSIDE CHANNEL LINE, EXCEPT AS NOTED

OBSTRUCTION BUOYS ARE MAINTAINED WHEN AN OBSTRUCTION IS A MENACE TO NAVIGATION

WEST VIRGINIA
KANAWHA CO.
CHARLESTON DISTRICT

WEST VIRGINIA
KANAWHA CO.
LOUDON DISTRICT

SET 45' FROM CHANNEL LINE AT N.P.

LEGEND

U. S. LIGHT	☀
DAYMARK	◆
CHANNEL BUOYS	
RED	○
BLACK	●
FLASHER BUOYS	
RED	☼
BLACK	✸

KANAWHA RIVER
AIDS TO NAVIGATION
ELK CHUTE

500   0   500   1000   1500
SCALE 1 IN. = 1000 FT

U. S. ENGINEER OFFICE, HUNTINGTON, W. VA.

DRAWN BY S.F.B.   FILE NO. 023-H3/6   DATE OCT. 1934

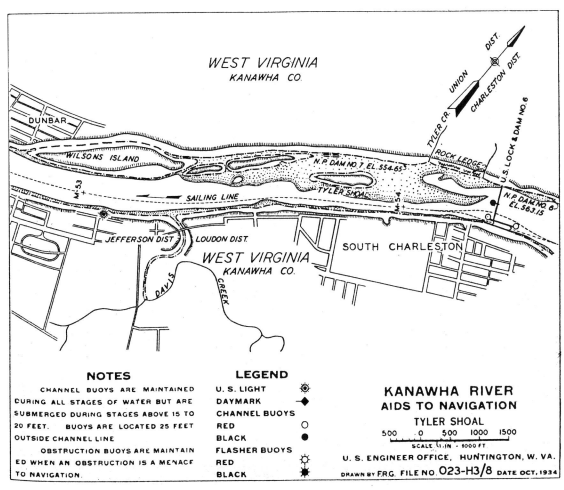

WEST VIRGINIA
KANAWHA CO.

DUNBAR

WILSONS ISLAND

SAILING LINE

N.P. DAM NO. 7 EL. 554.65

TYLER SHOAL

TYLER CR.

ROCK LEDGE

U.S. LOCK & DAM NO. 6

N.P. DAM NO. 6 EL. 563.15

UNION DIST.
CHARLESTON DIST.

JEFFERSON DIST   LOUDON DIST.

WEST VIRGINIA
KANAWHA CO.

SOUTH CHARLESTON

DAVIS CREEK

NOTES

CHANNEL BUOYS ARE MAINTAINED DURING ALL STAGES OF WATER BUT ARE SUBMERGED DURING STAGES ABOVE 15 TO 20 FEET.   BUOYS ARE LOCATED 25 FEET OUTSIDE CHANNEL LINE

OBSTRUCTION BUOYS ARE MAINTAINED WHEN AN OBSTRUCTION IS A MENACE TO NAVIGATION.

LEGEND

U. S. LIGHT	☀
DAYMARK	◆
CHANNEL BUOYS	
RED	○
BLACK	●
FLASHER BUOYS	
RED	☼
BLACK	✸

KANAWHA RIVER
AIDS TO NAVIGATION
TYLER SHOAL

500   0   500   1000   1500
SCALE 1 IN. = 1000 FT

U. S. ENGINEER OFFICE, HUNTINGTON, W. VA.

DRAWN BY F.R.G.   FILE NO. 023-H3/8   DATE OCT. 1934

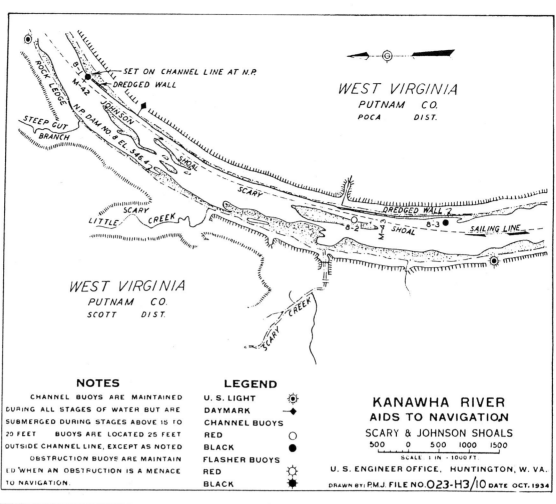

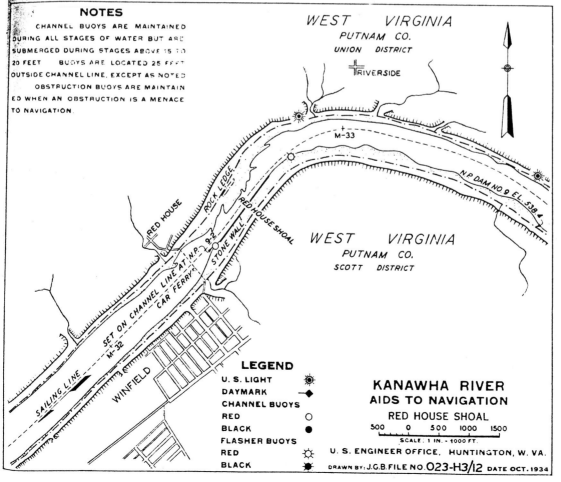